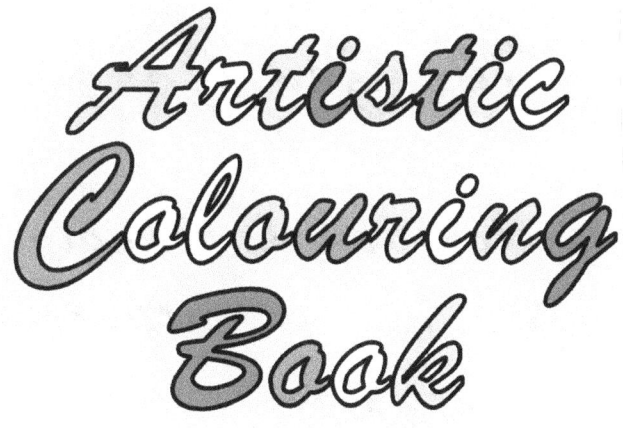

All is a point of imagination. Until where our reality expands depends on how far our imagination can bring us. Colour is a joy! Thank you all for purchasing my colouring book! My passion are flowers, that's why here you can find unique designs of a diverse range of beautiful flowers which you can bring to life with your own imagination. Creativity is meditation.

Let your mind flow and colour!

Share with us your amazing ideas on our Facebook page <u>www.facebook.com/ArtisticColoringBook</u> and be a part of our colour community! In this book, you can find also creative kaleidoscopes and mandalas which can help you unleash the potential of your mind and bring joy and peace to everyone.

Don't forget to leave a review!

Thank you!
Sincerely yours
Milena Sladkova

The Zen Garden

Take a deep slow breath. Imagine you are in a peaceful garden. You are sitting under an apple tree. Your eyes are closed. It's the beginning of spring when life comes to awake again. The grass is high and gently touches your bare feet. There are beautiful colourful flowers all around you. You can hear the cheerful tweeting of distant birds. They sing a song of happiness. Little insects buzz lazily somewhere near you. You can feel the warmness of the sun on your skin. It's not too hot. You are protected by the shade of the tree. There is a perfect balance! The shadows of the leaves flicker around you like little butterflies. You can see the shine even through your closed eyes. You never needed to see the beauty of the world because the beauty was always inside you. The air is filled with the sweet smell of apple blossoms. You take a deep breath. You breathe in all that peace that is surrounding you and it fills your mind and your soul. Gently you open your eyes and you smile. You bring peace.

Happy colouring!

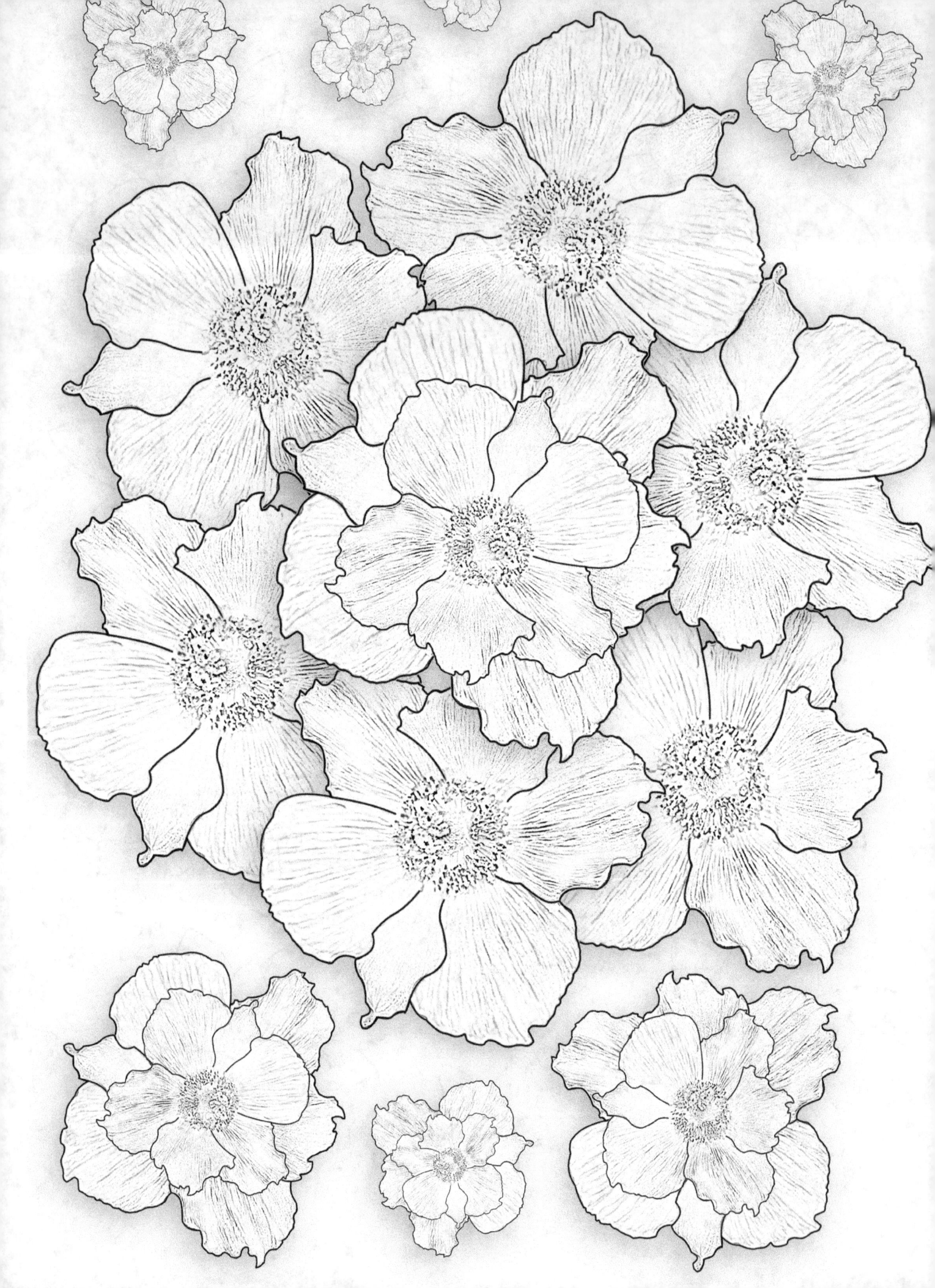

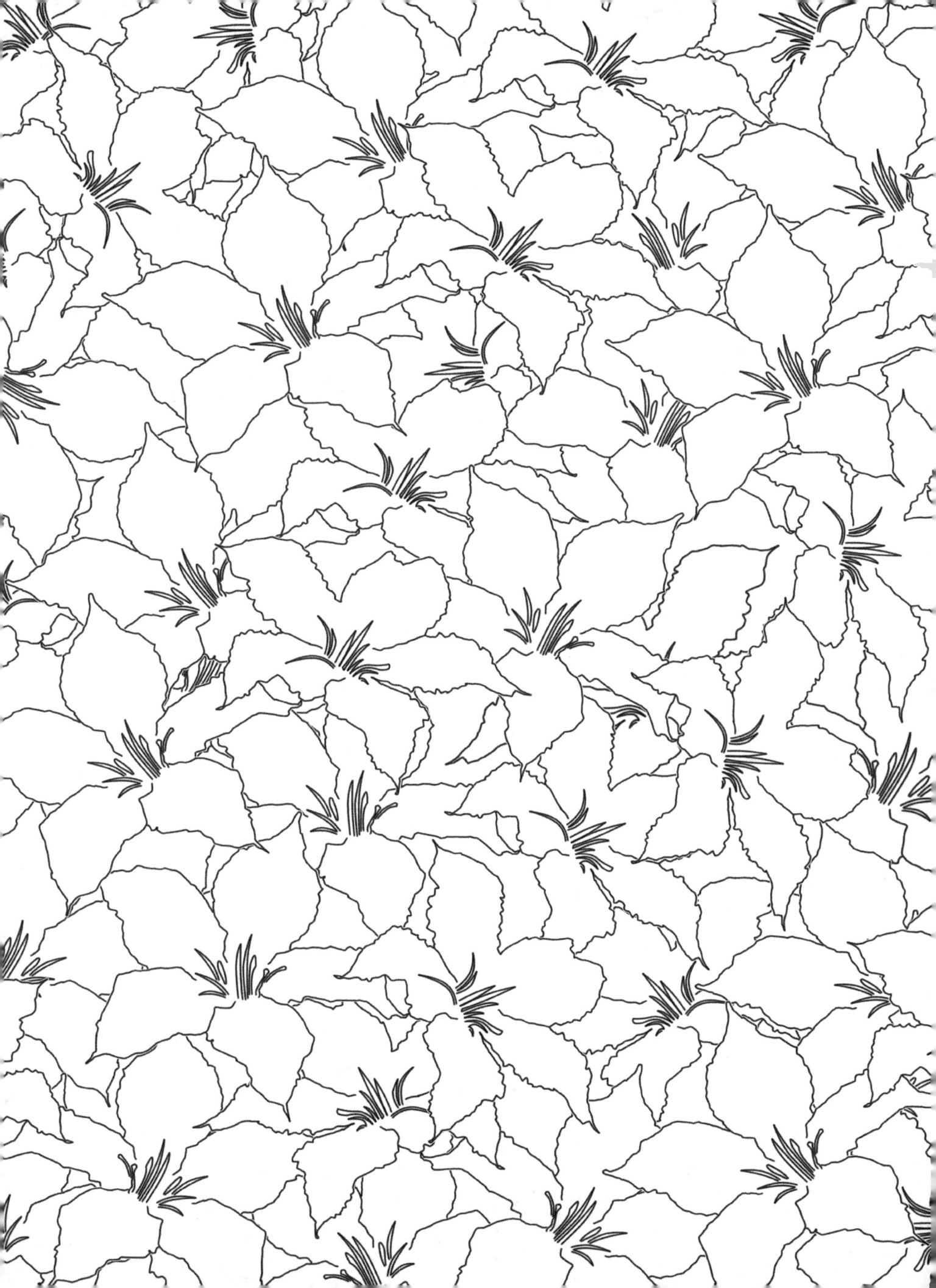

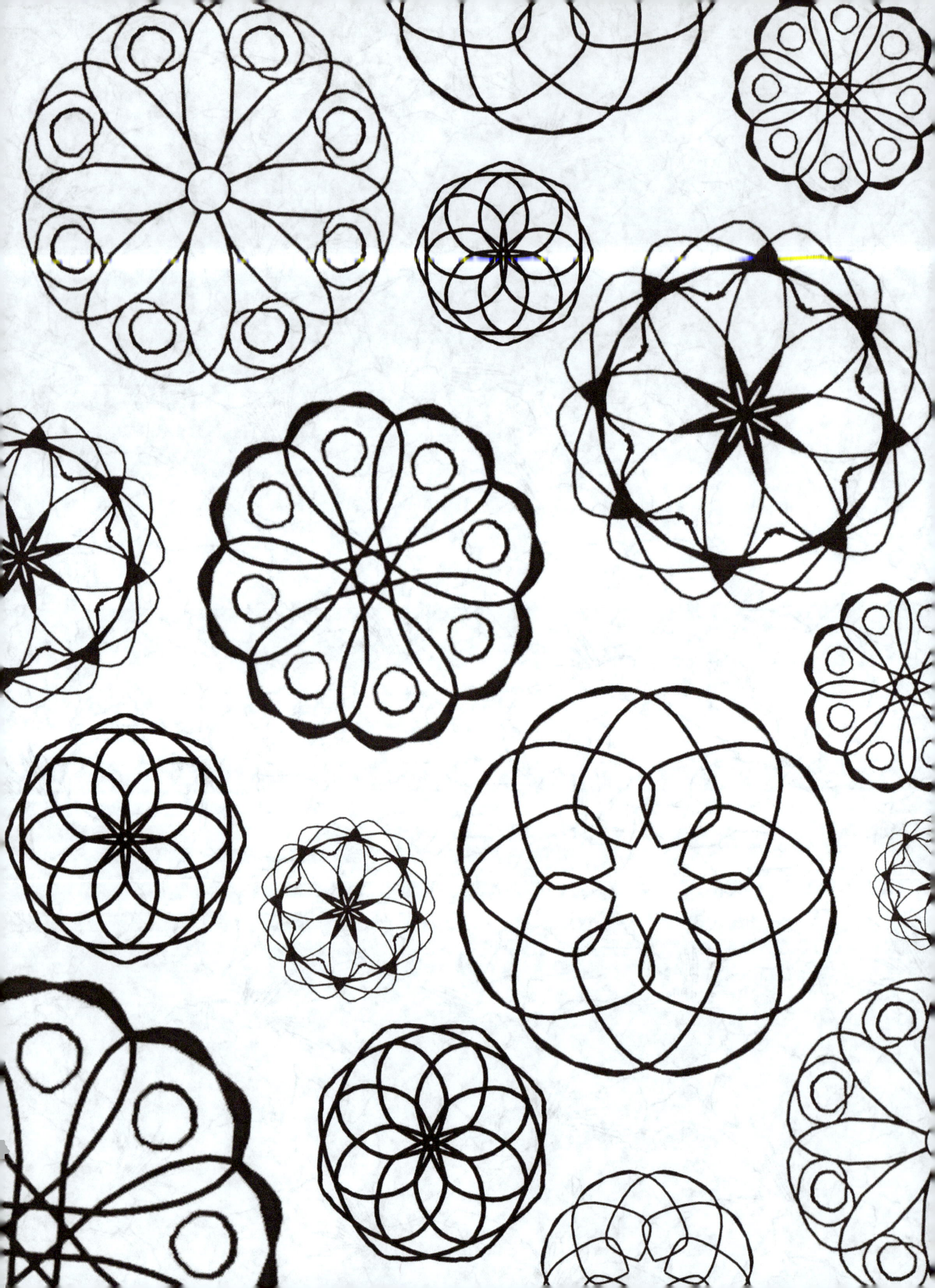

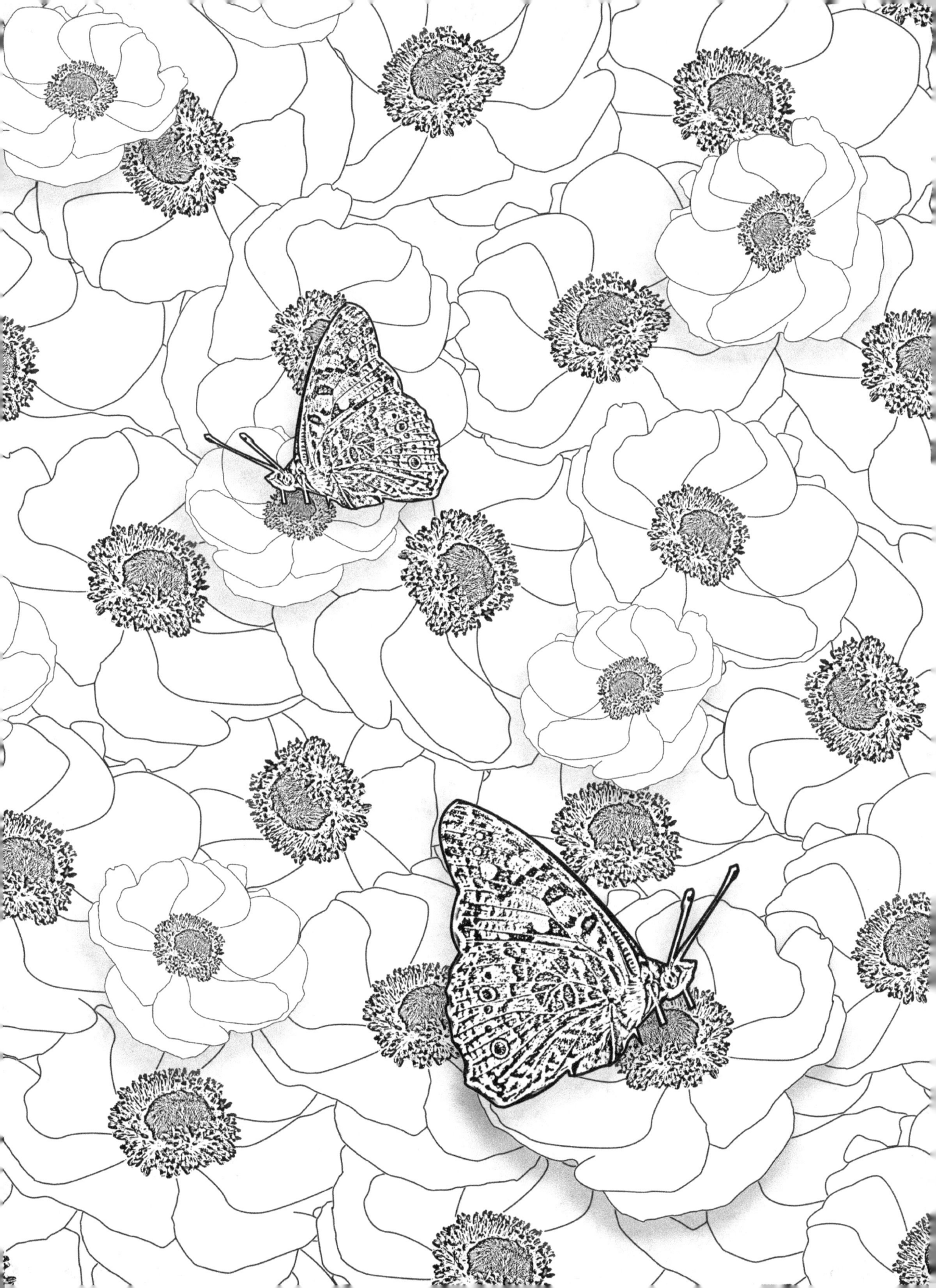

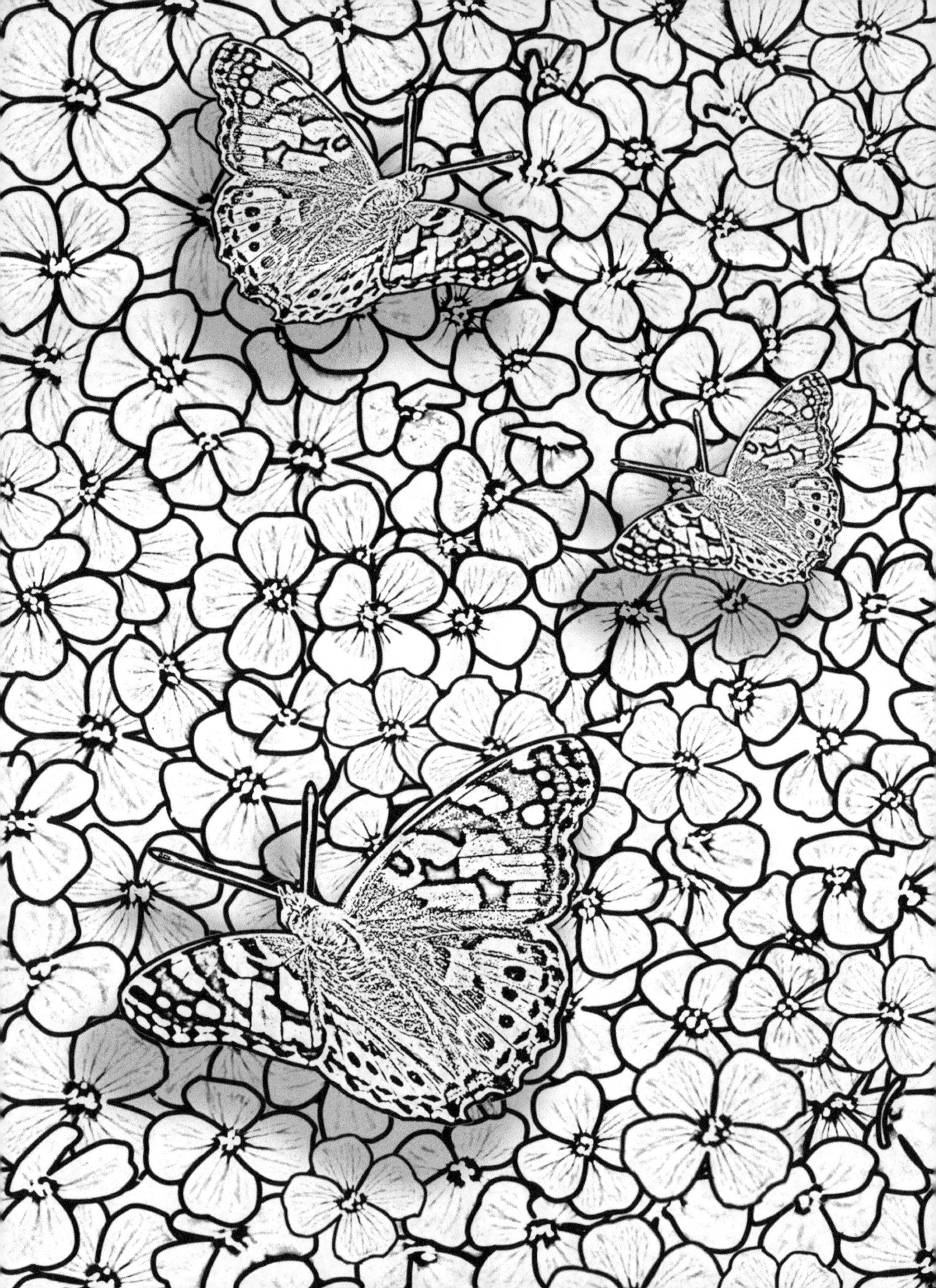

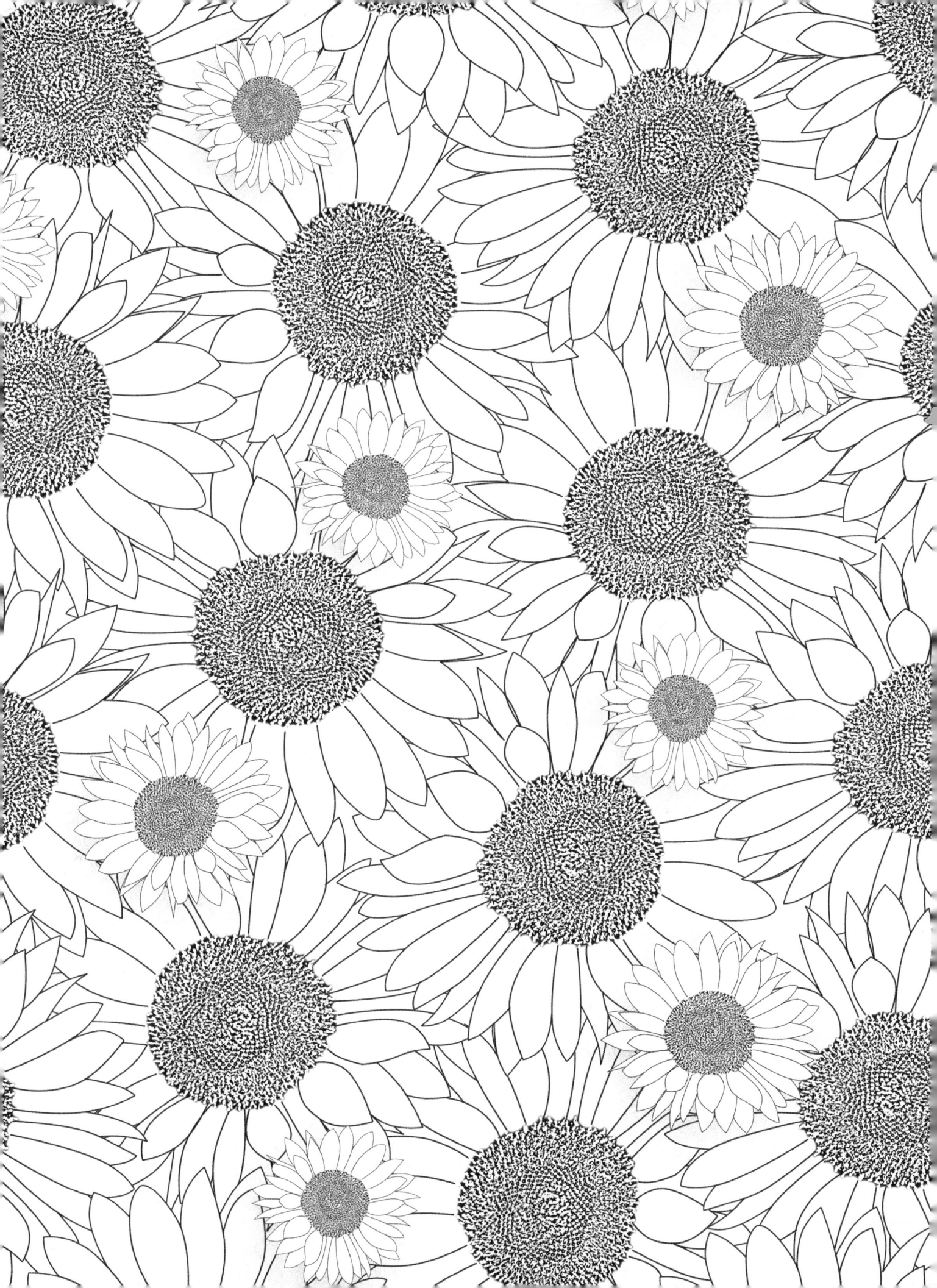

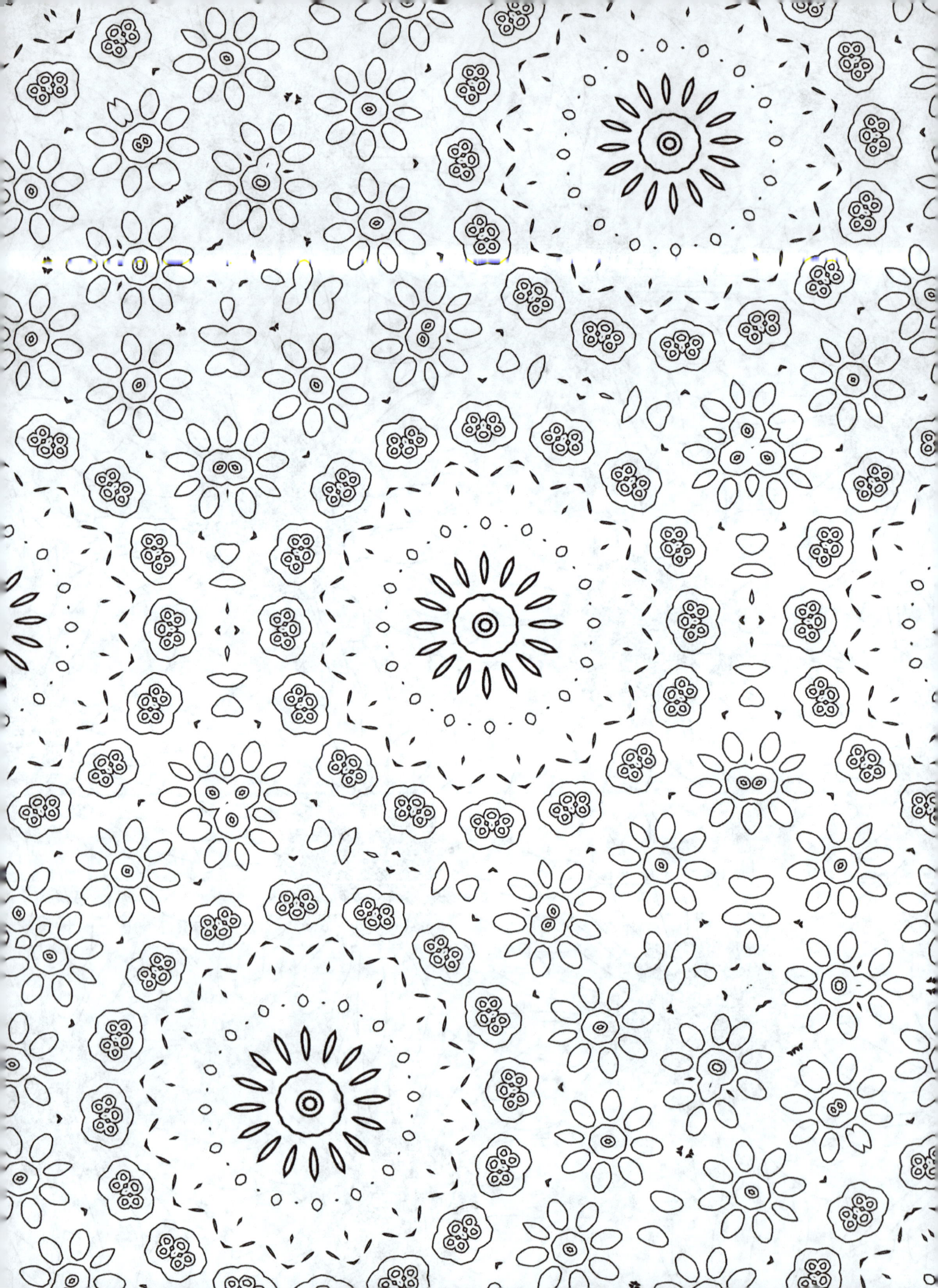

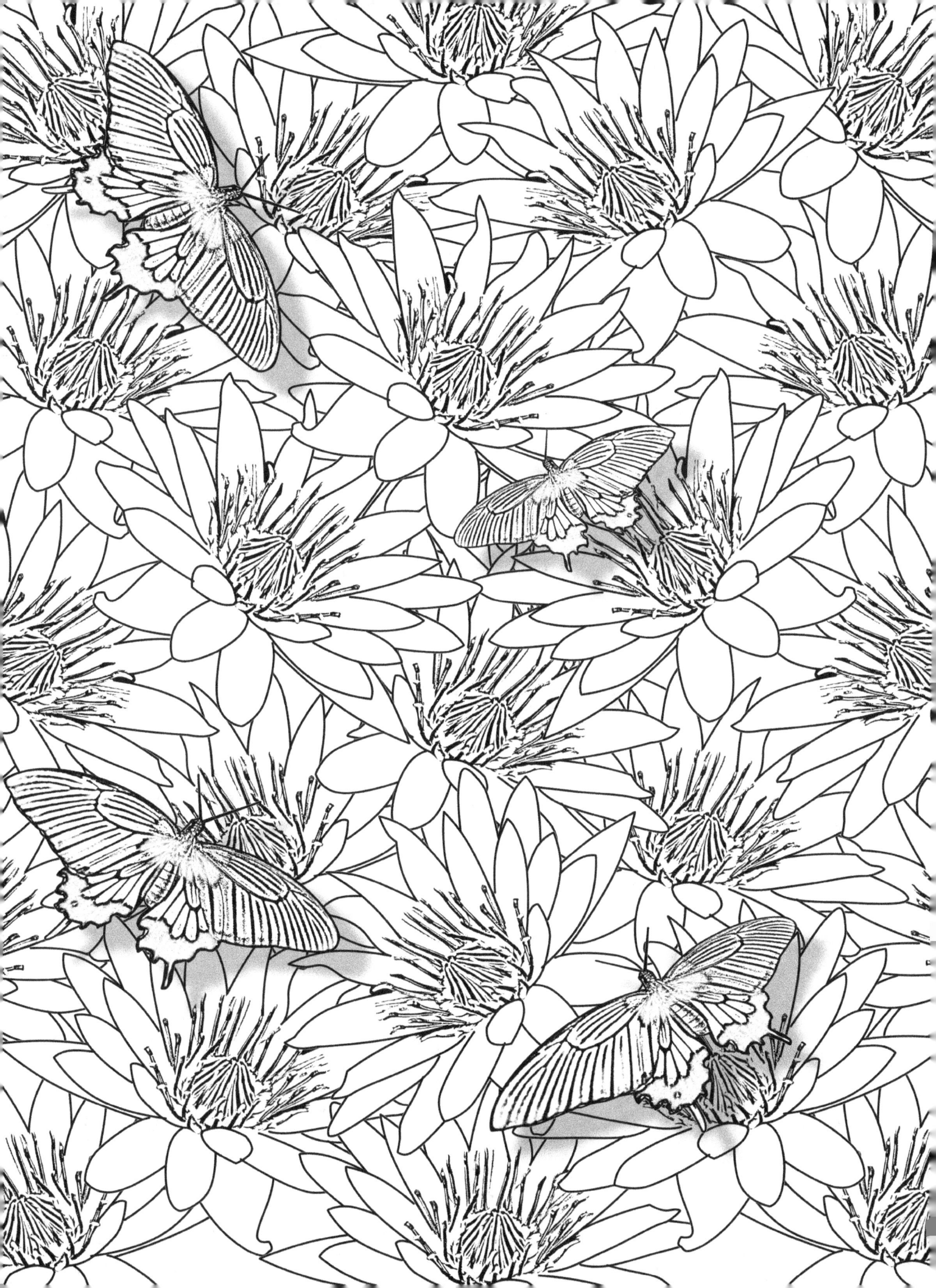

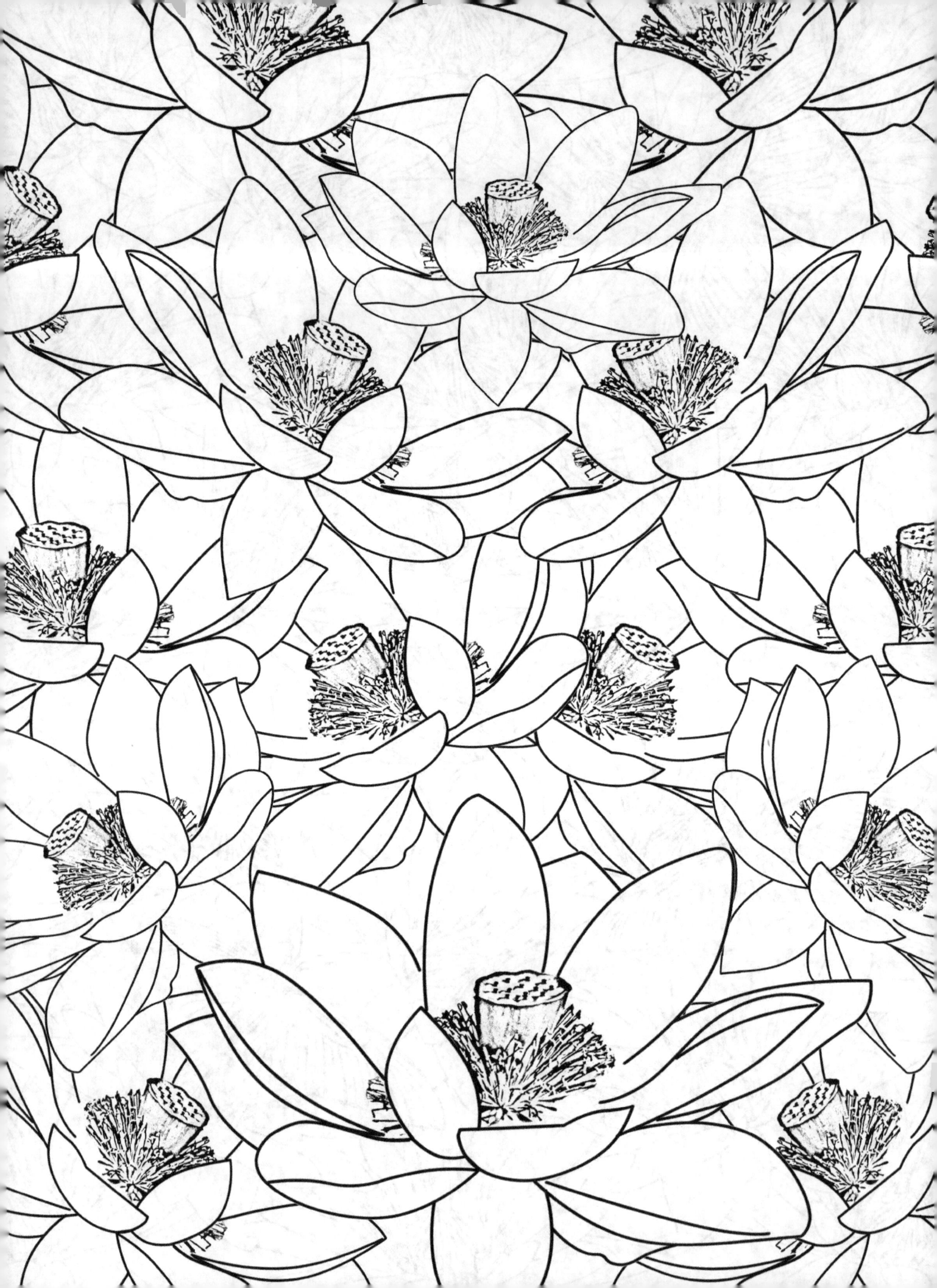

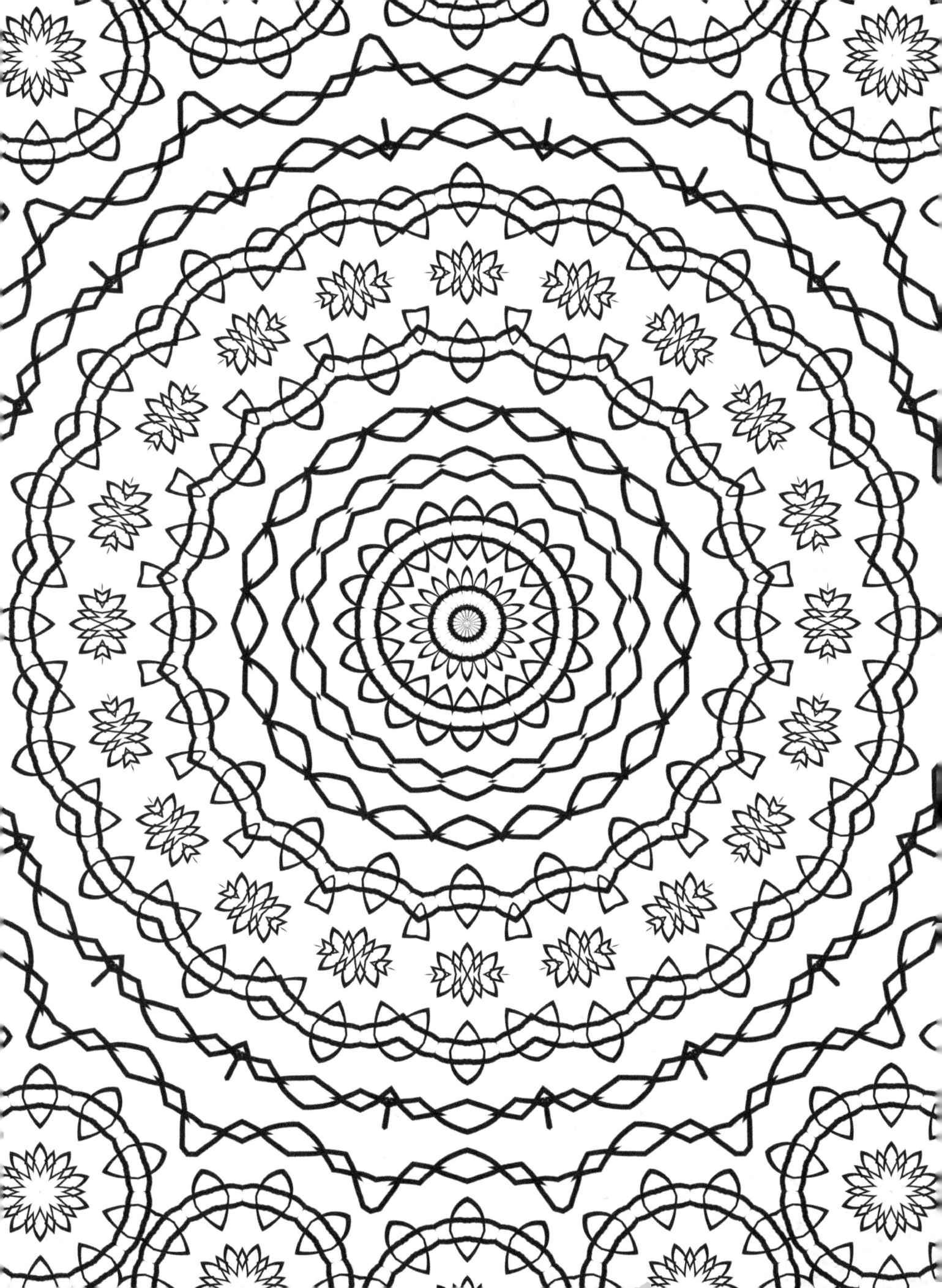

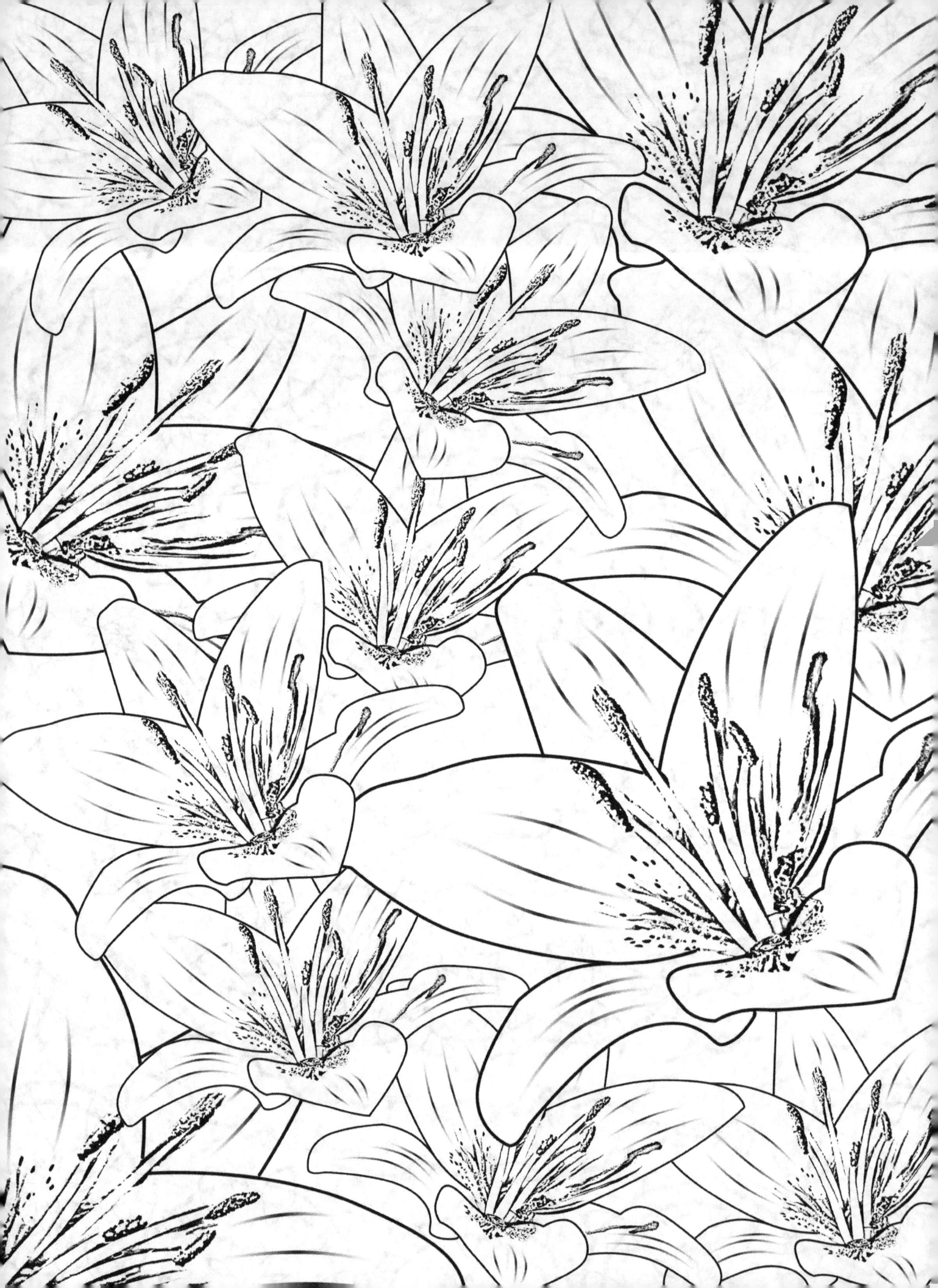

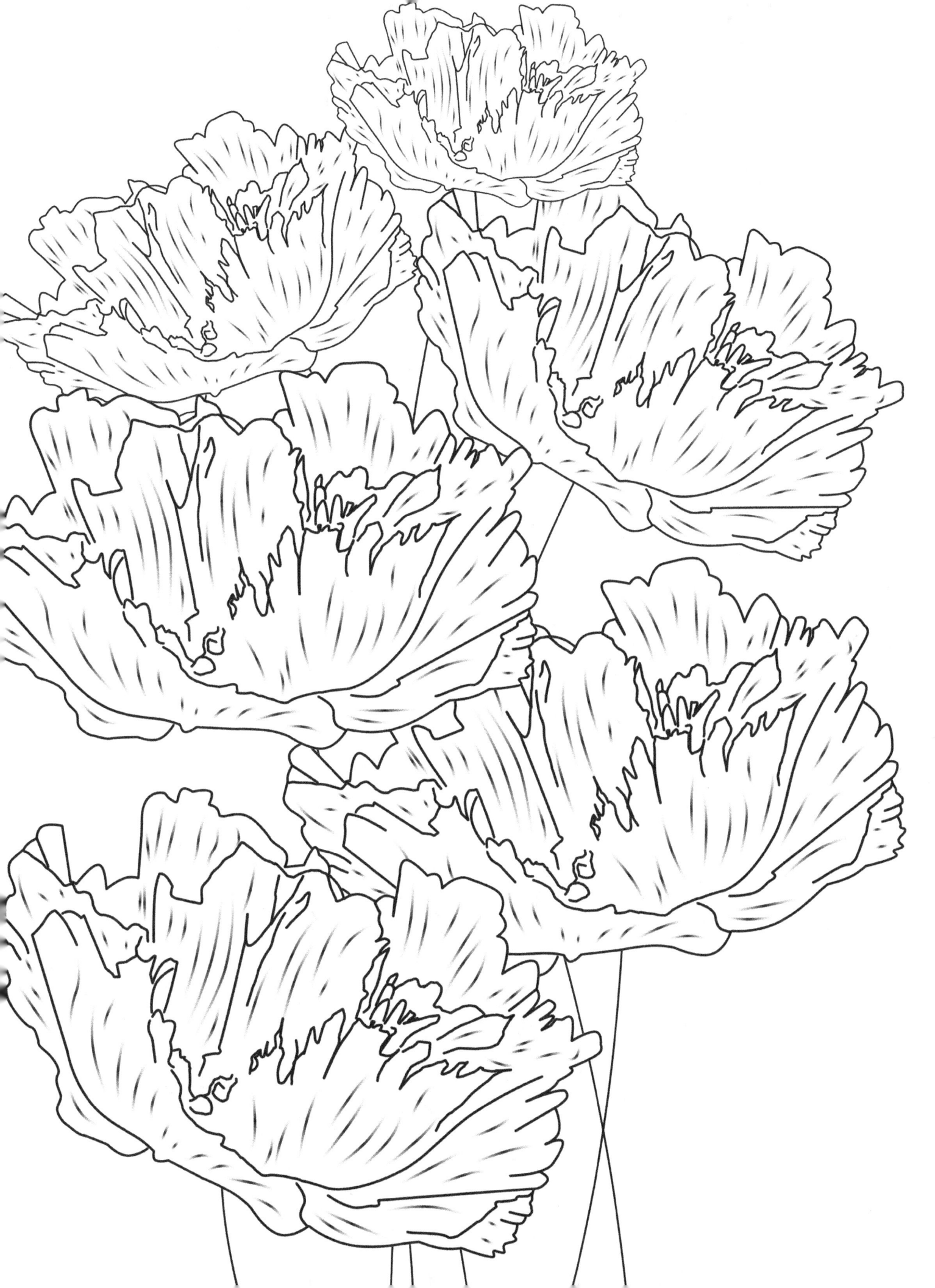

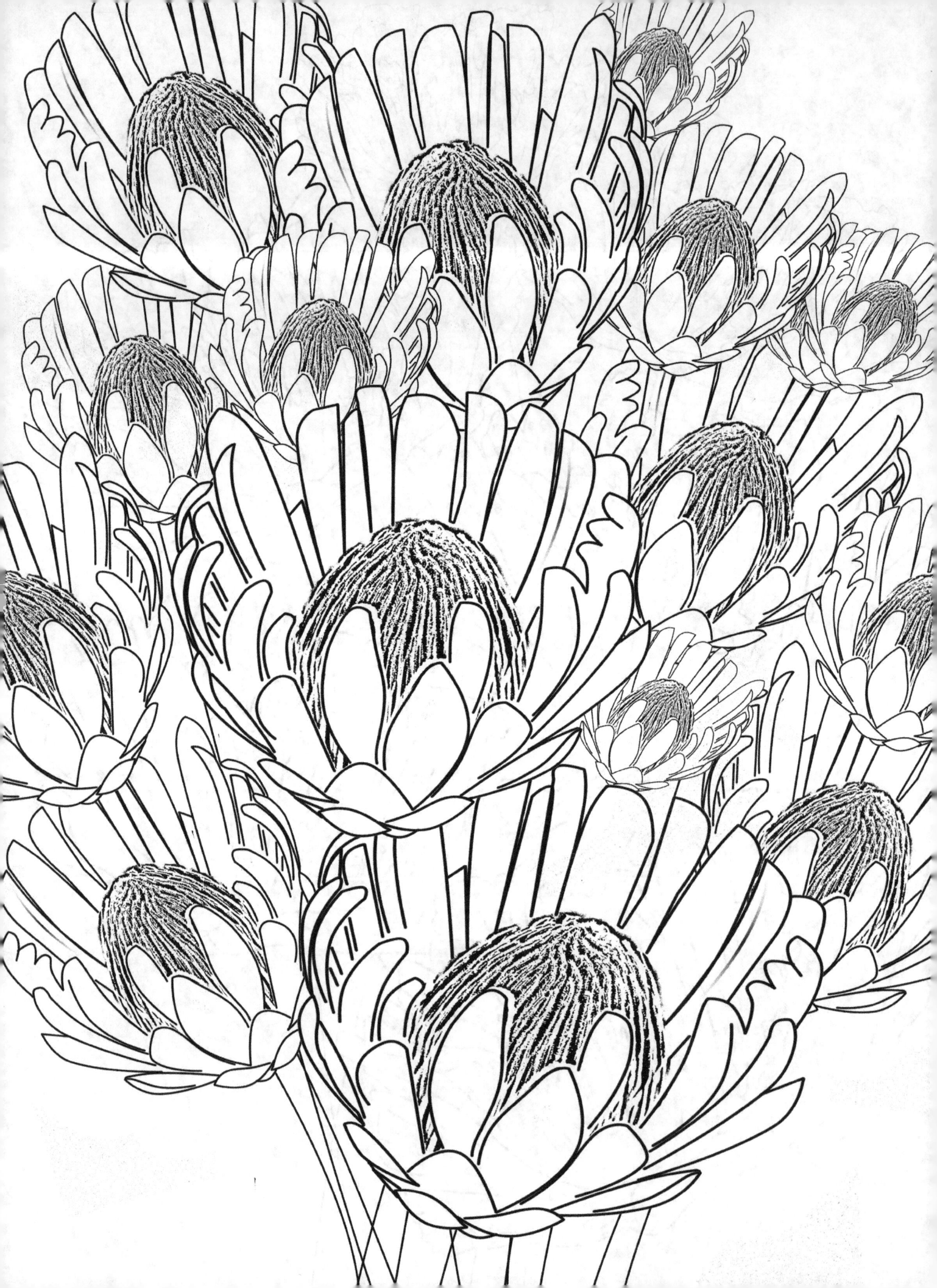

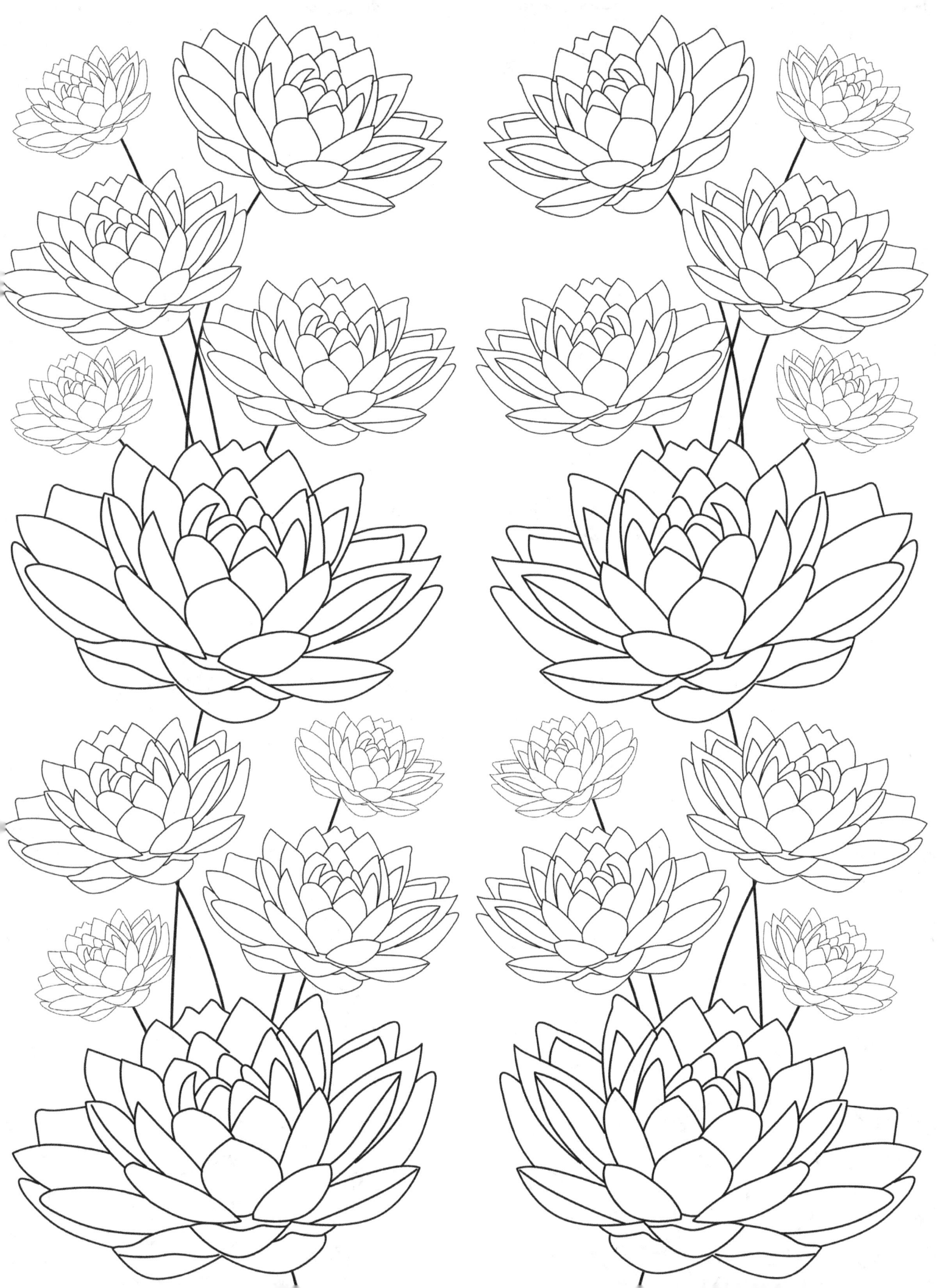

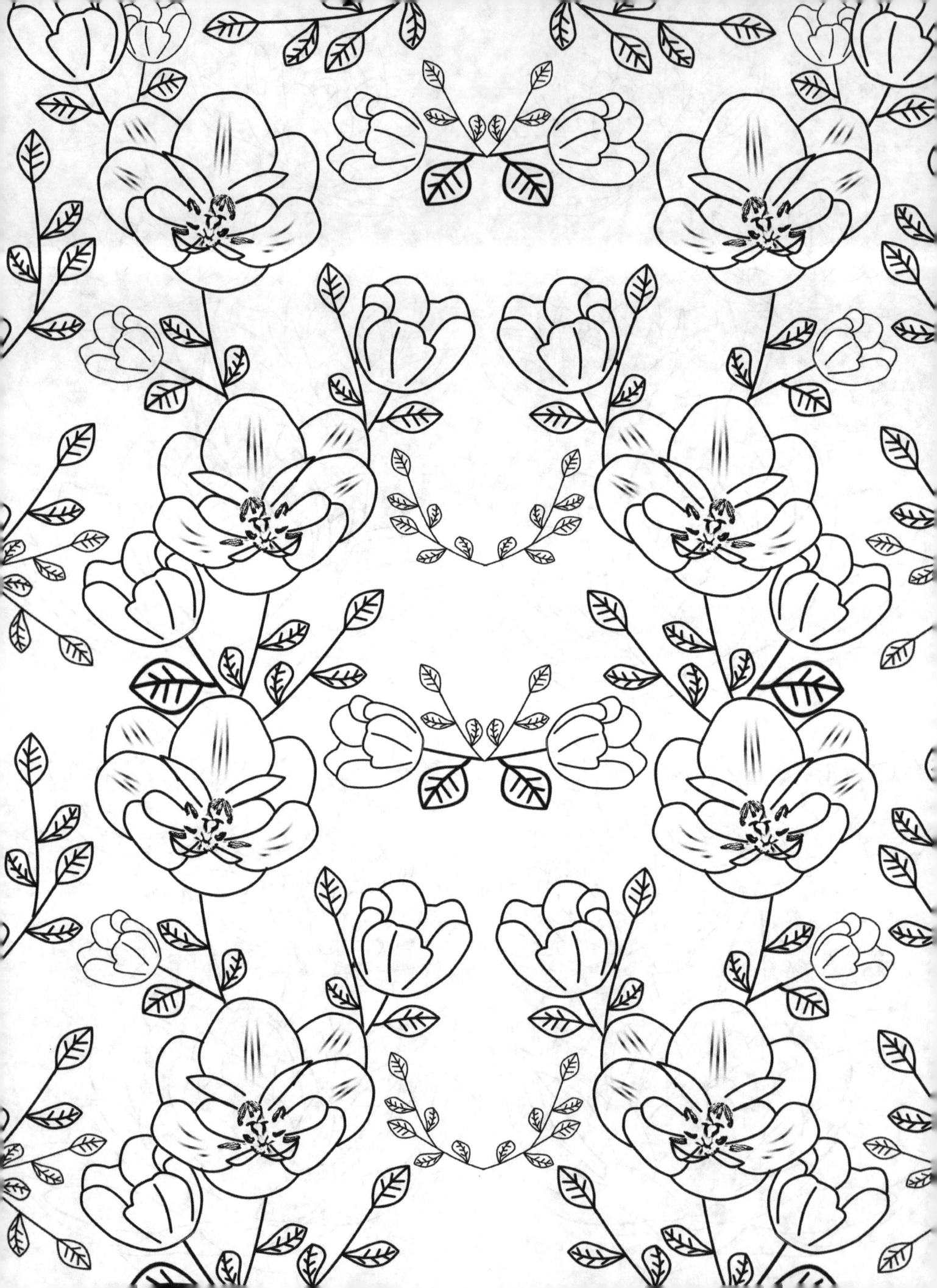

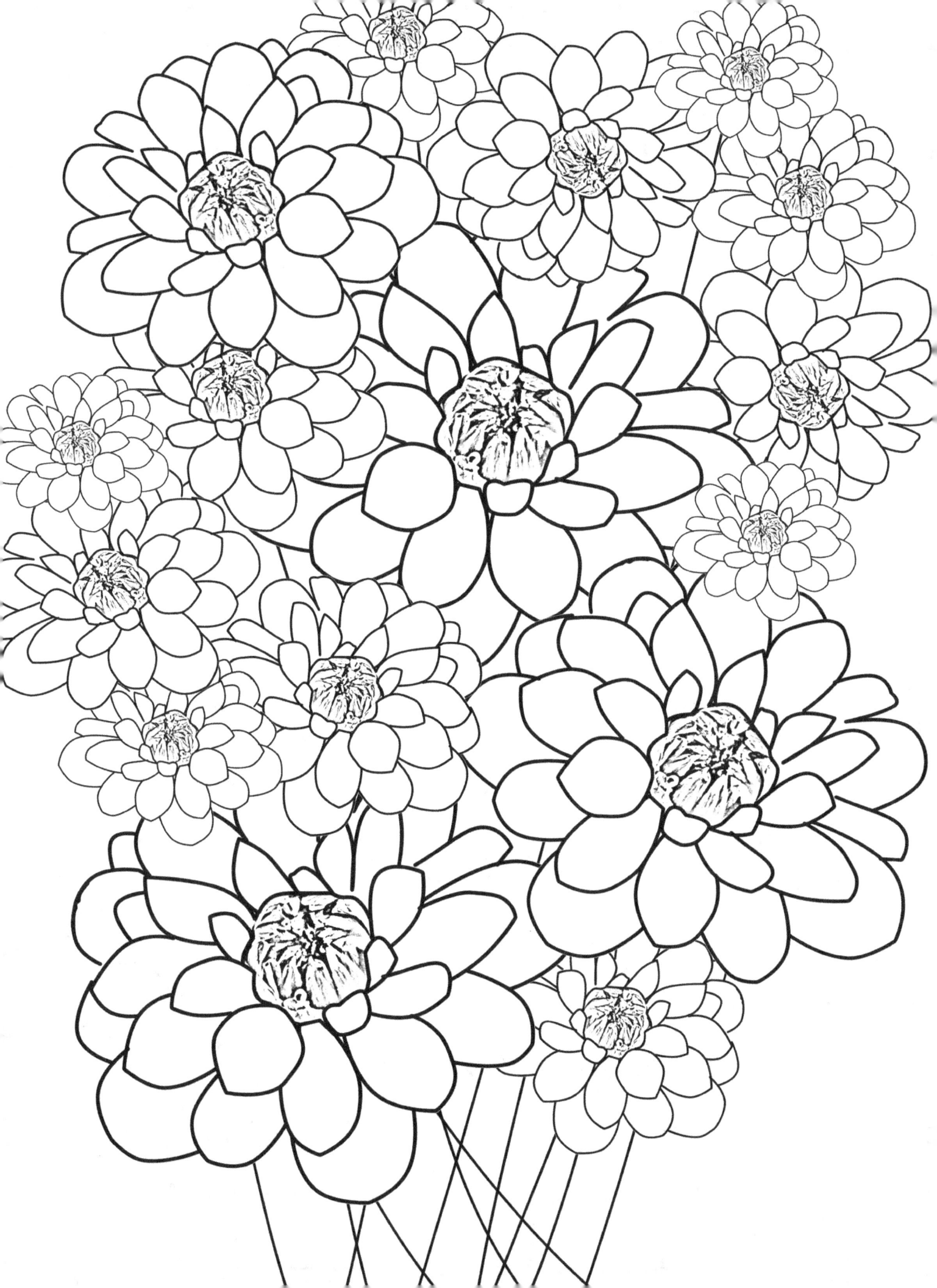

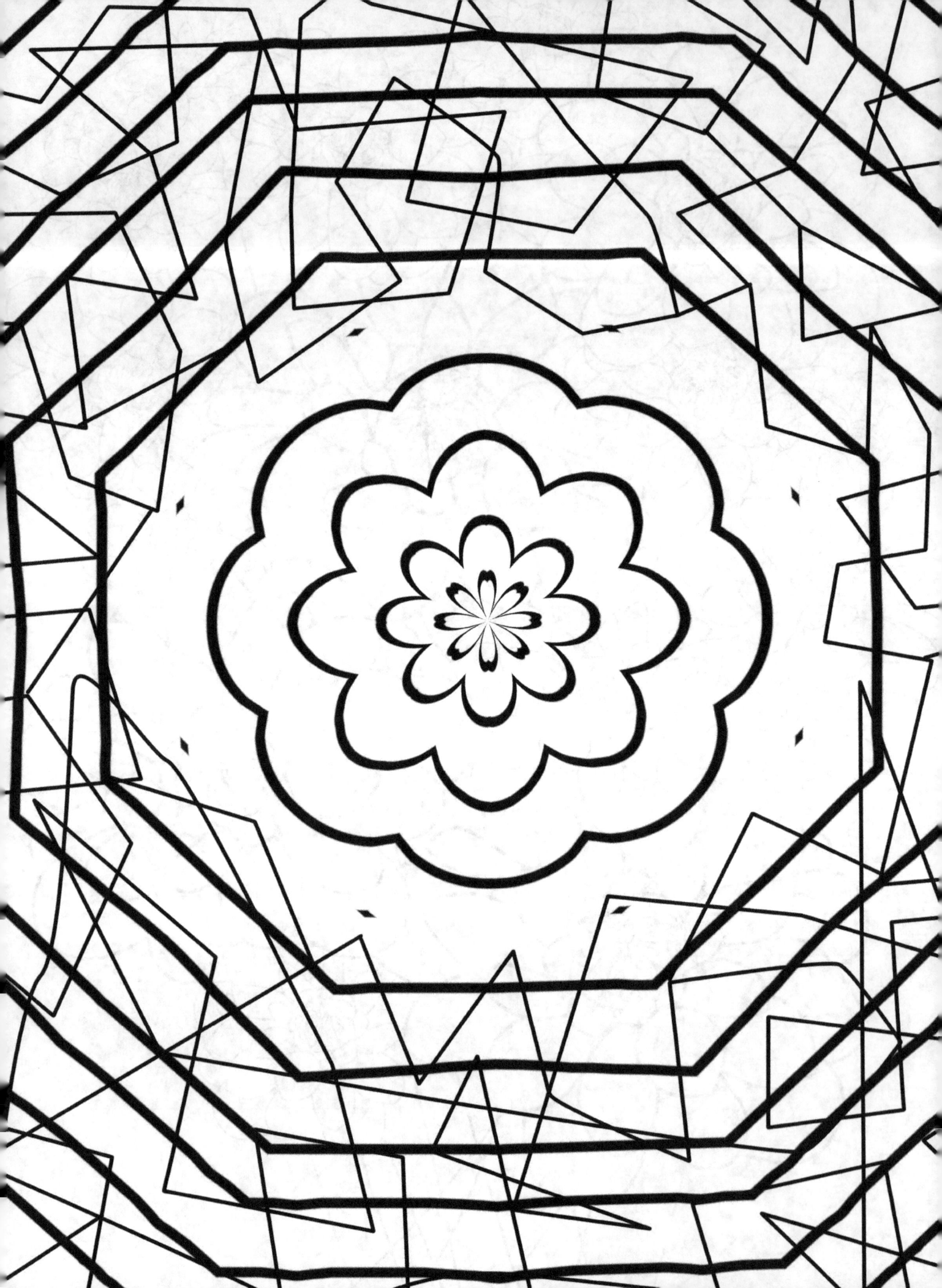

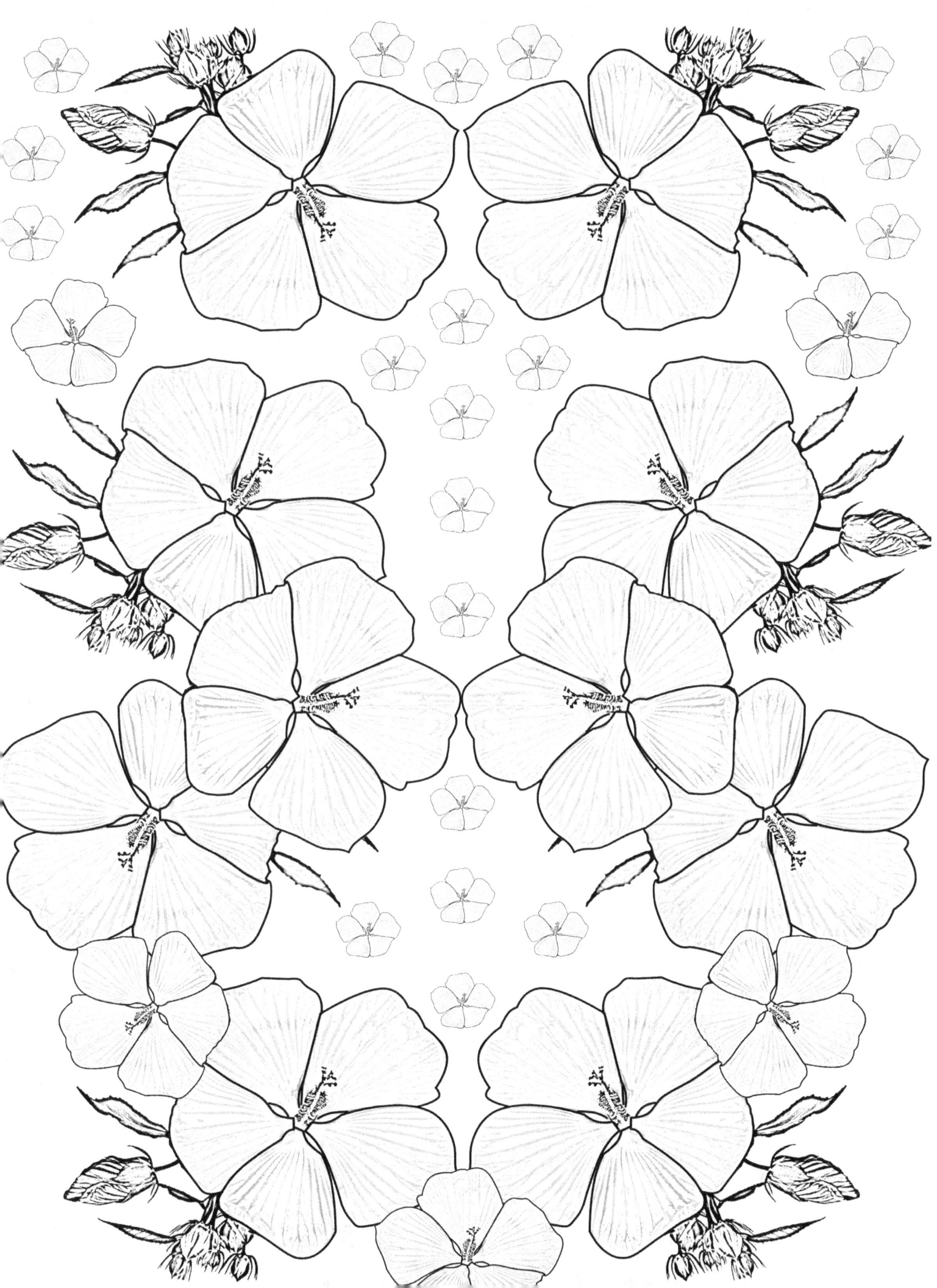

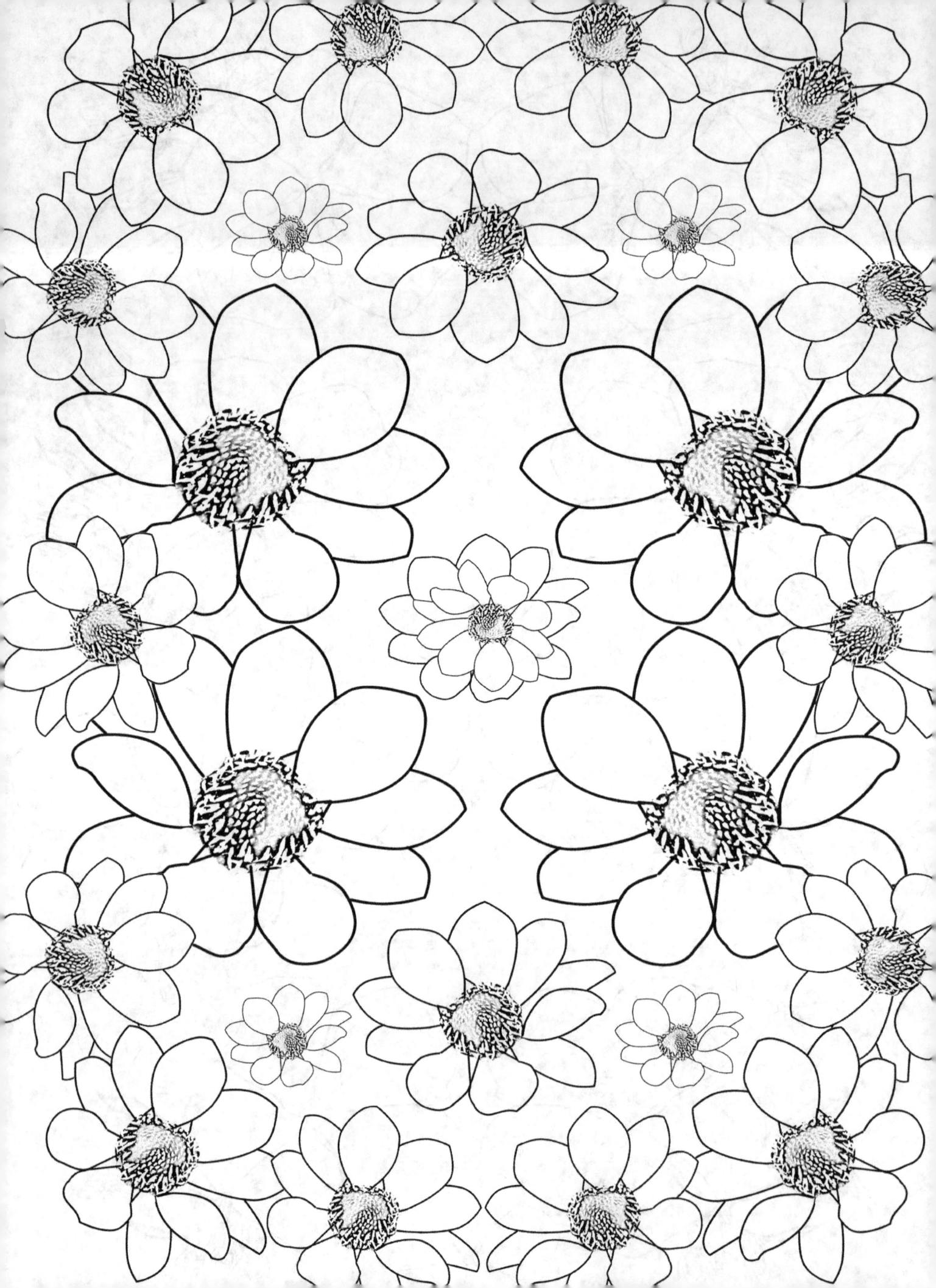

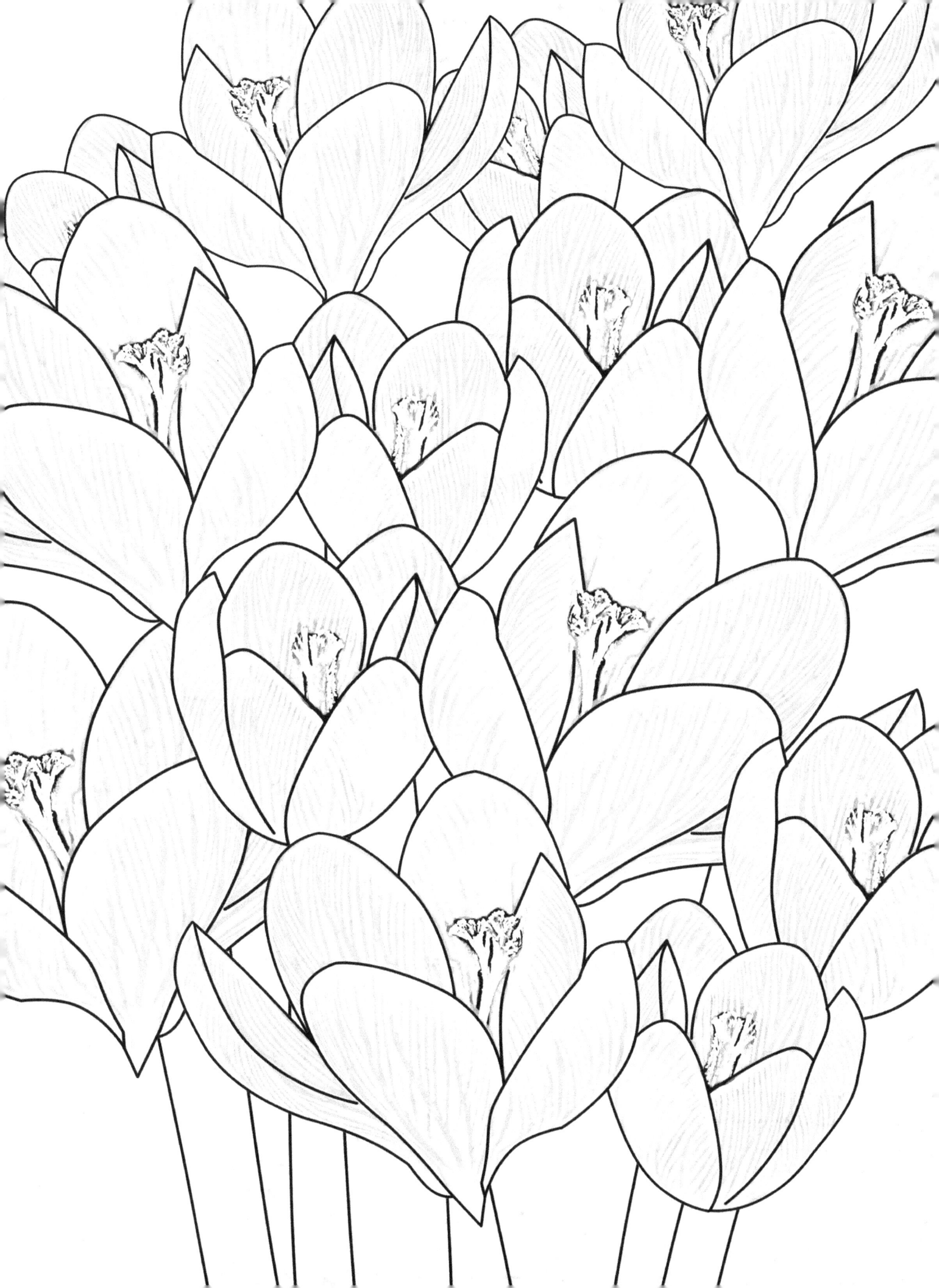

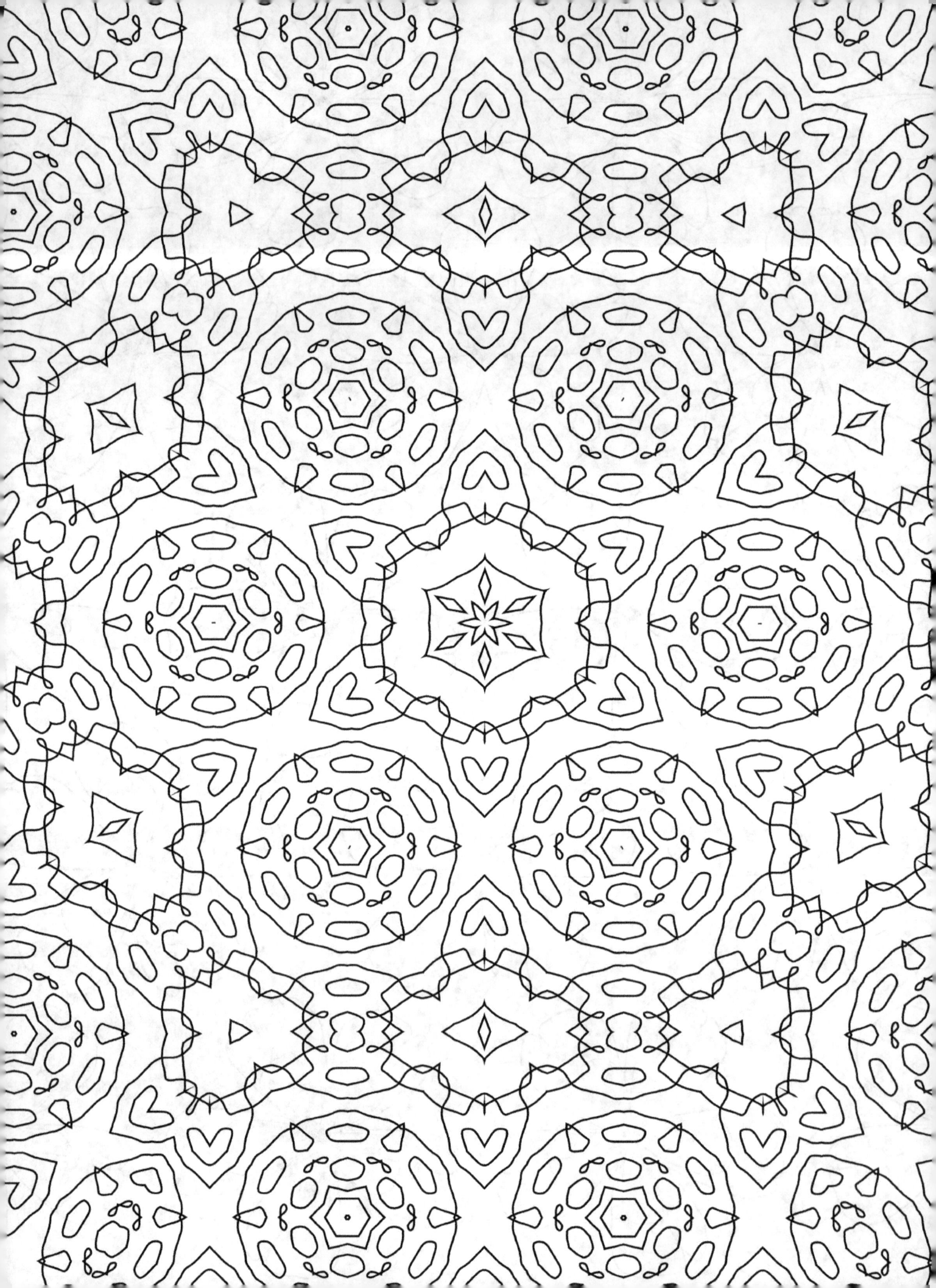

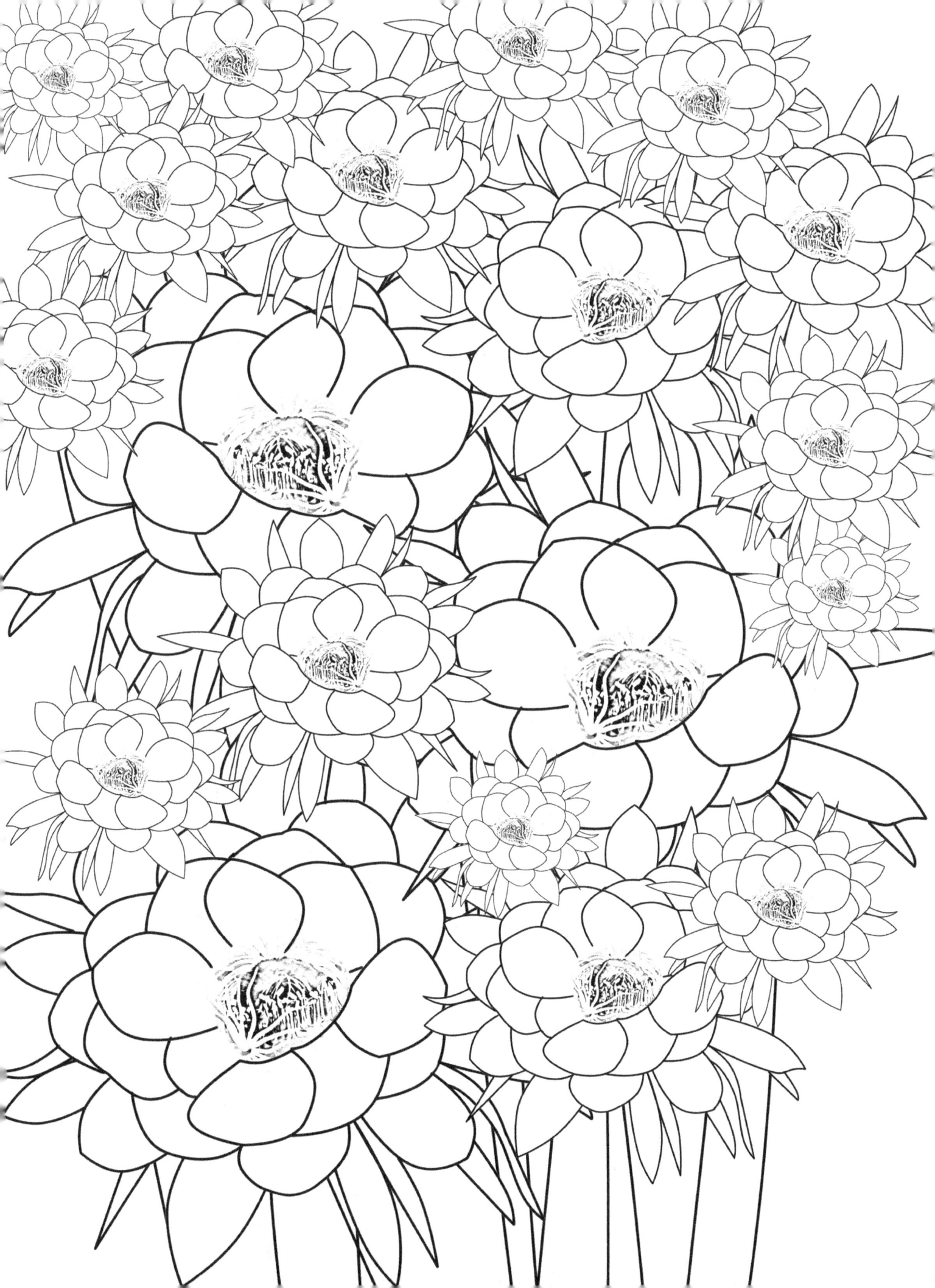

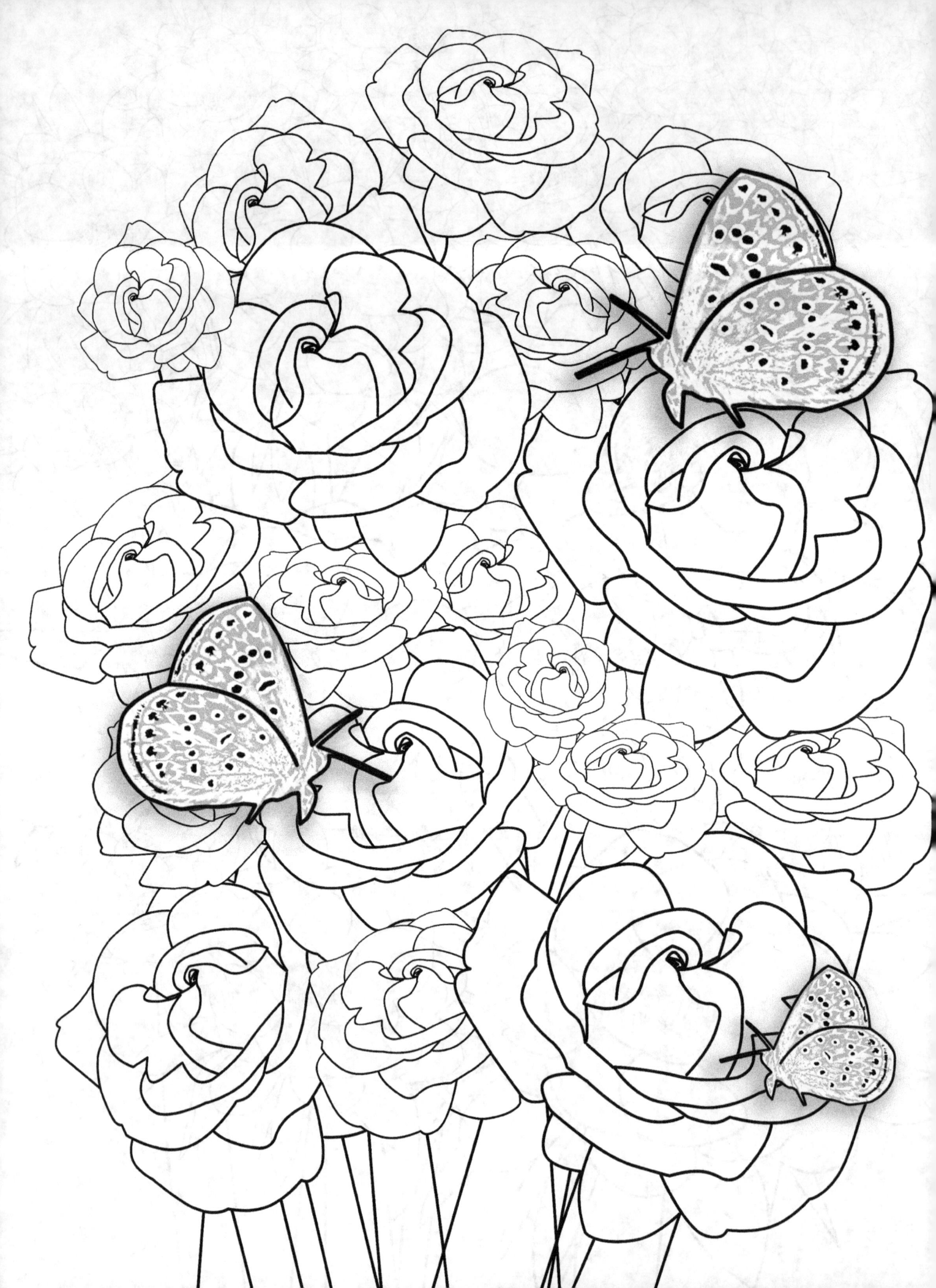

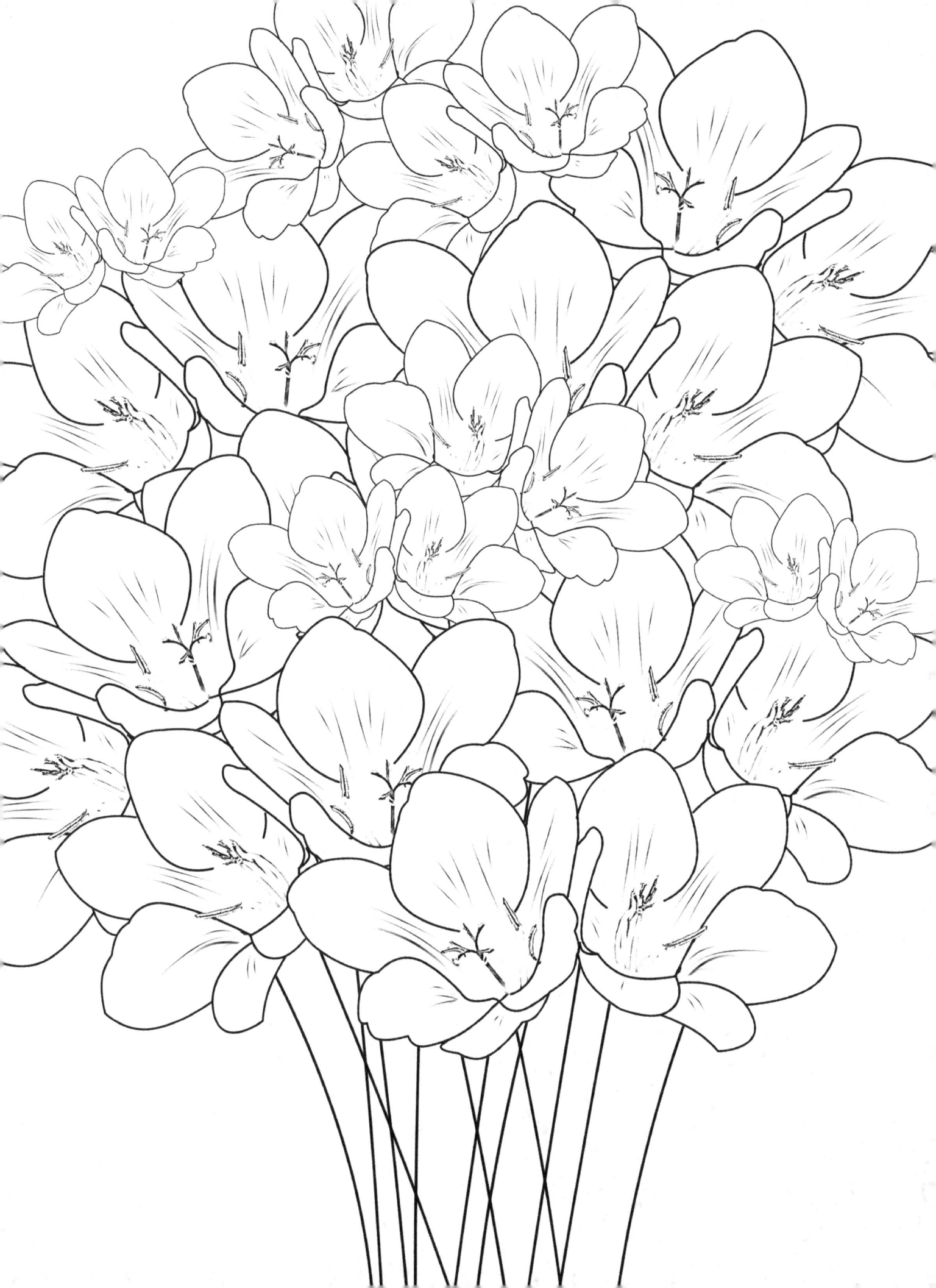

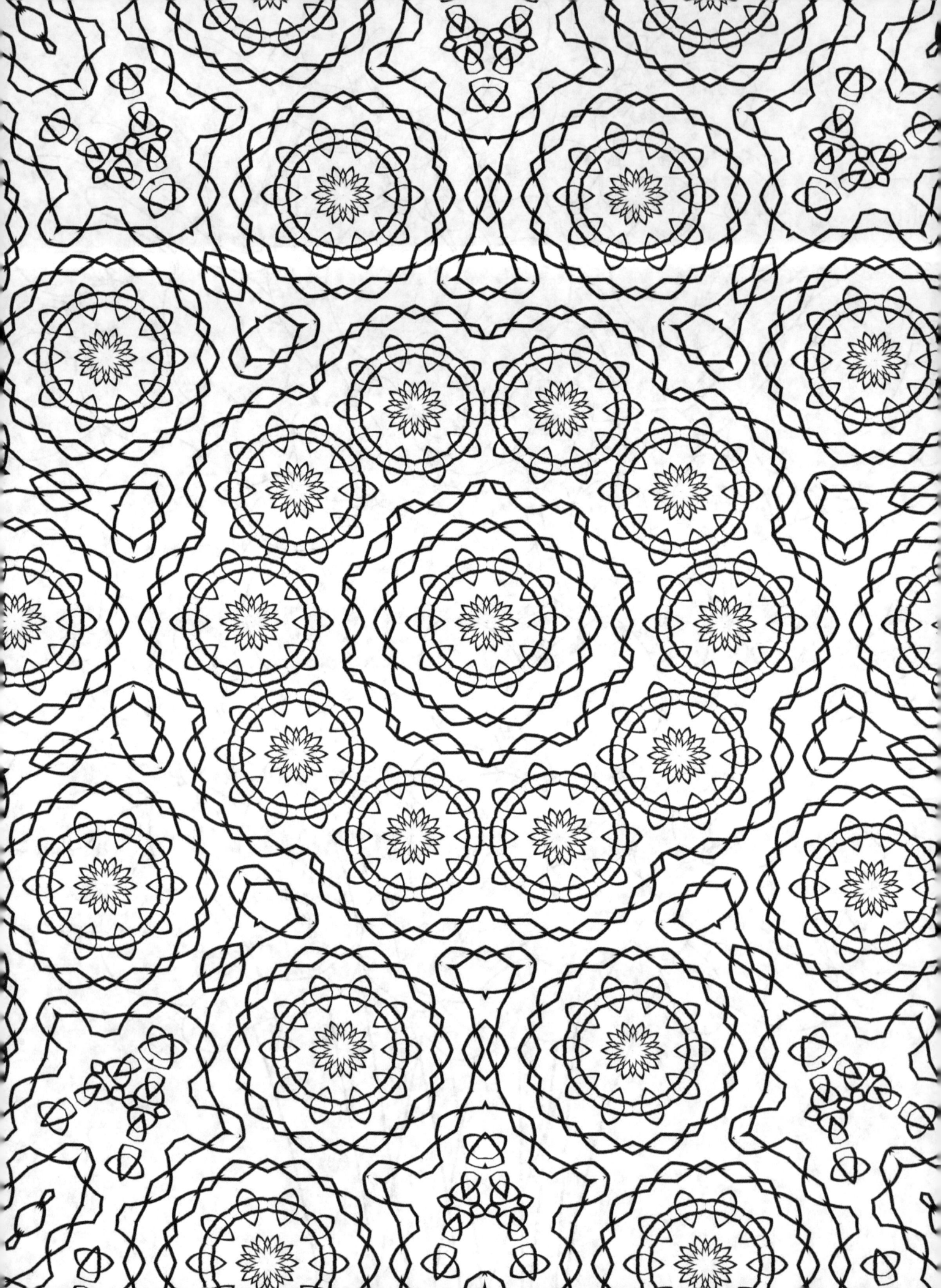

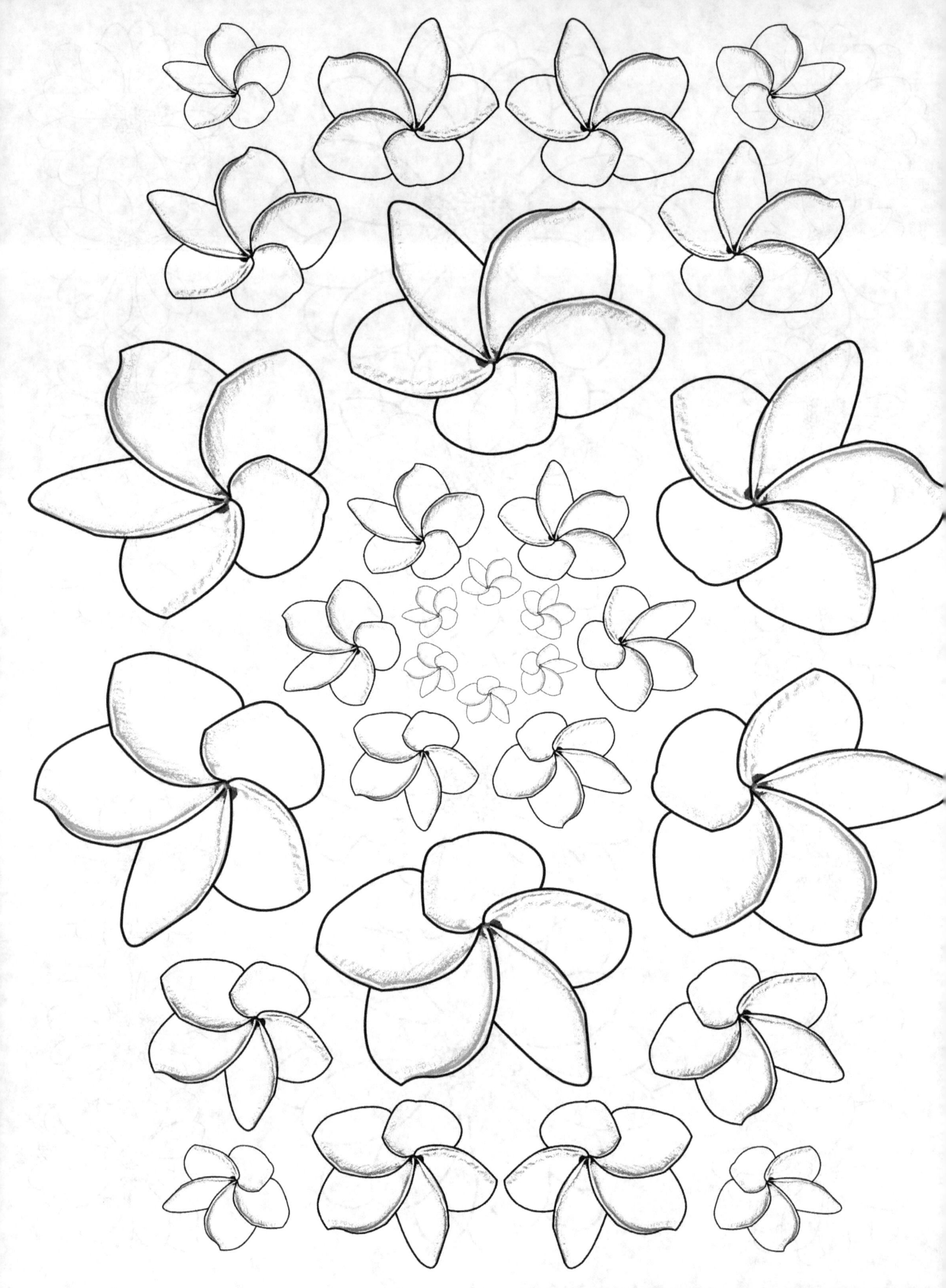

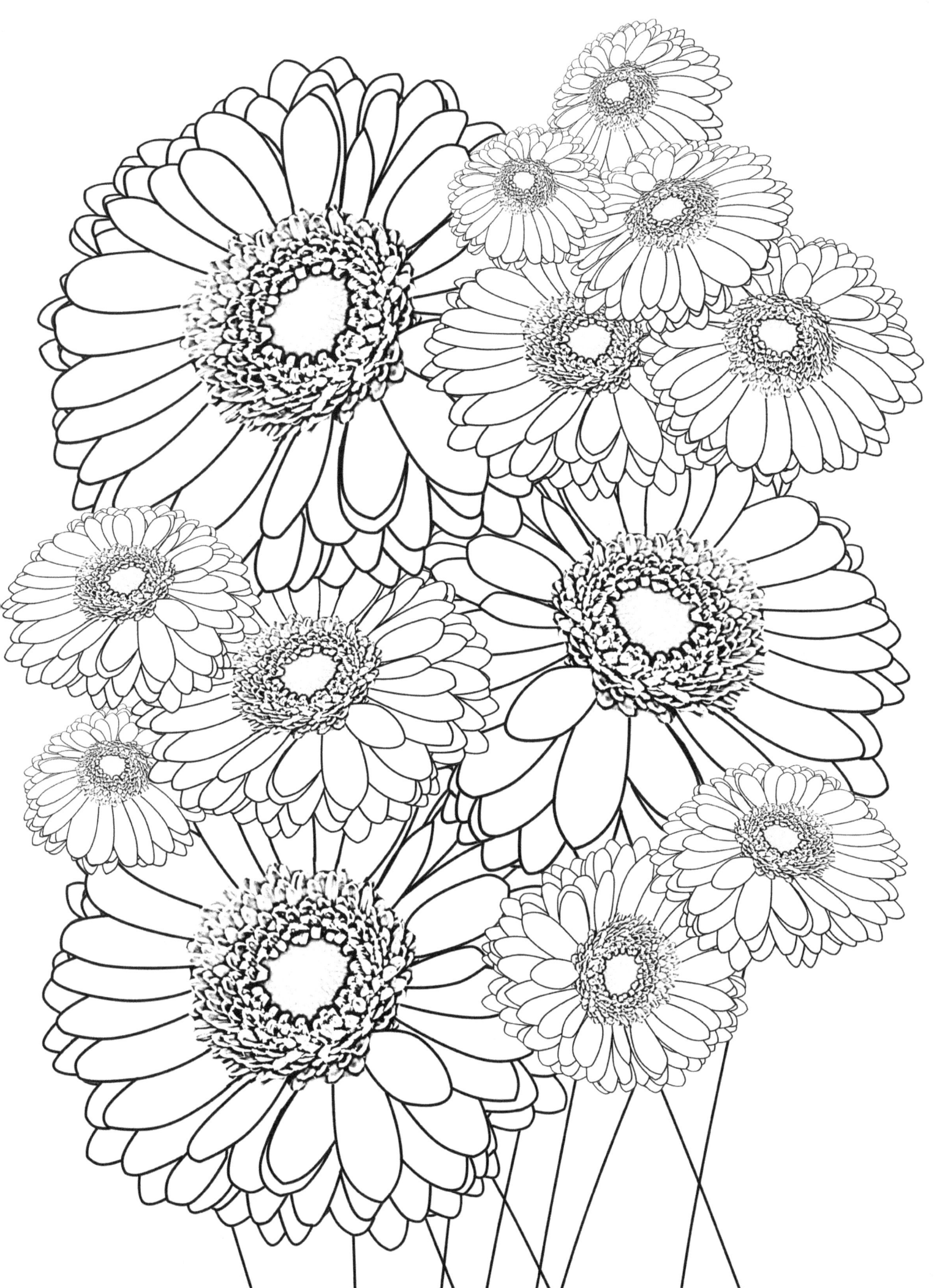

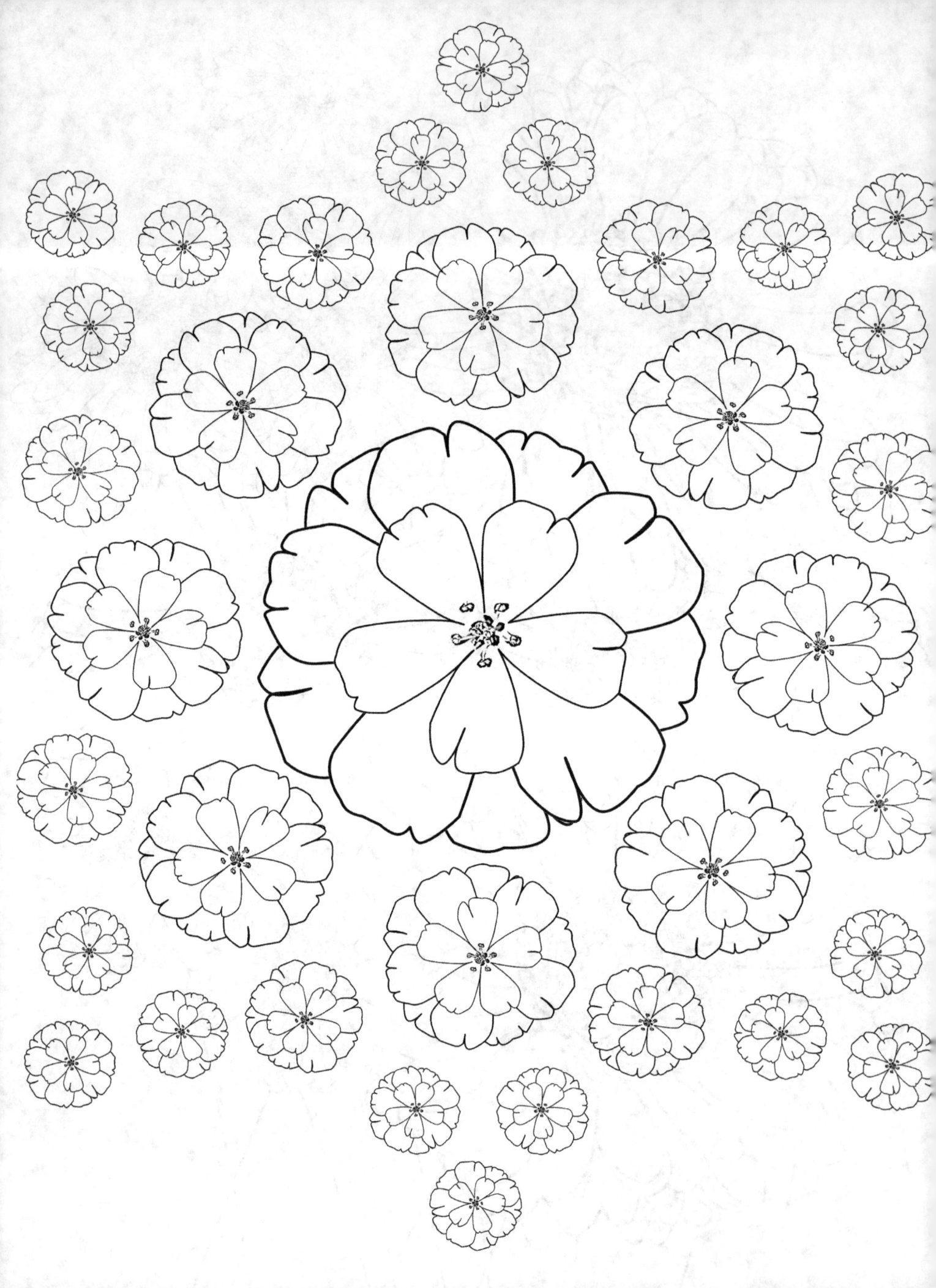

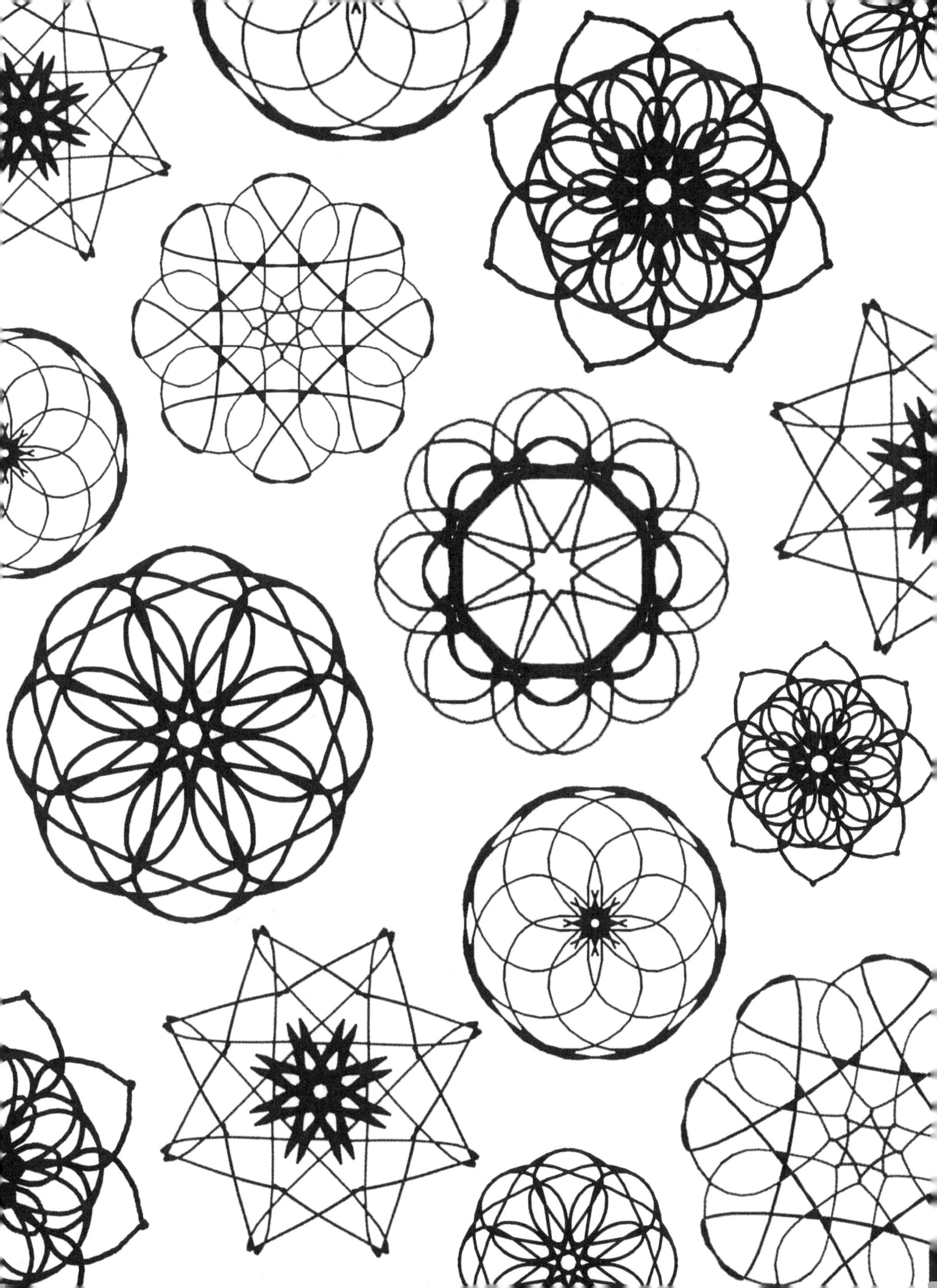

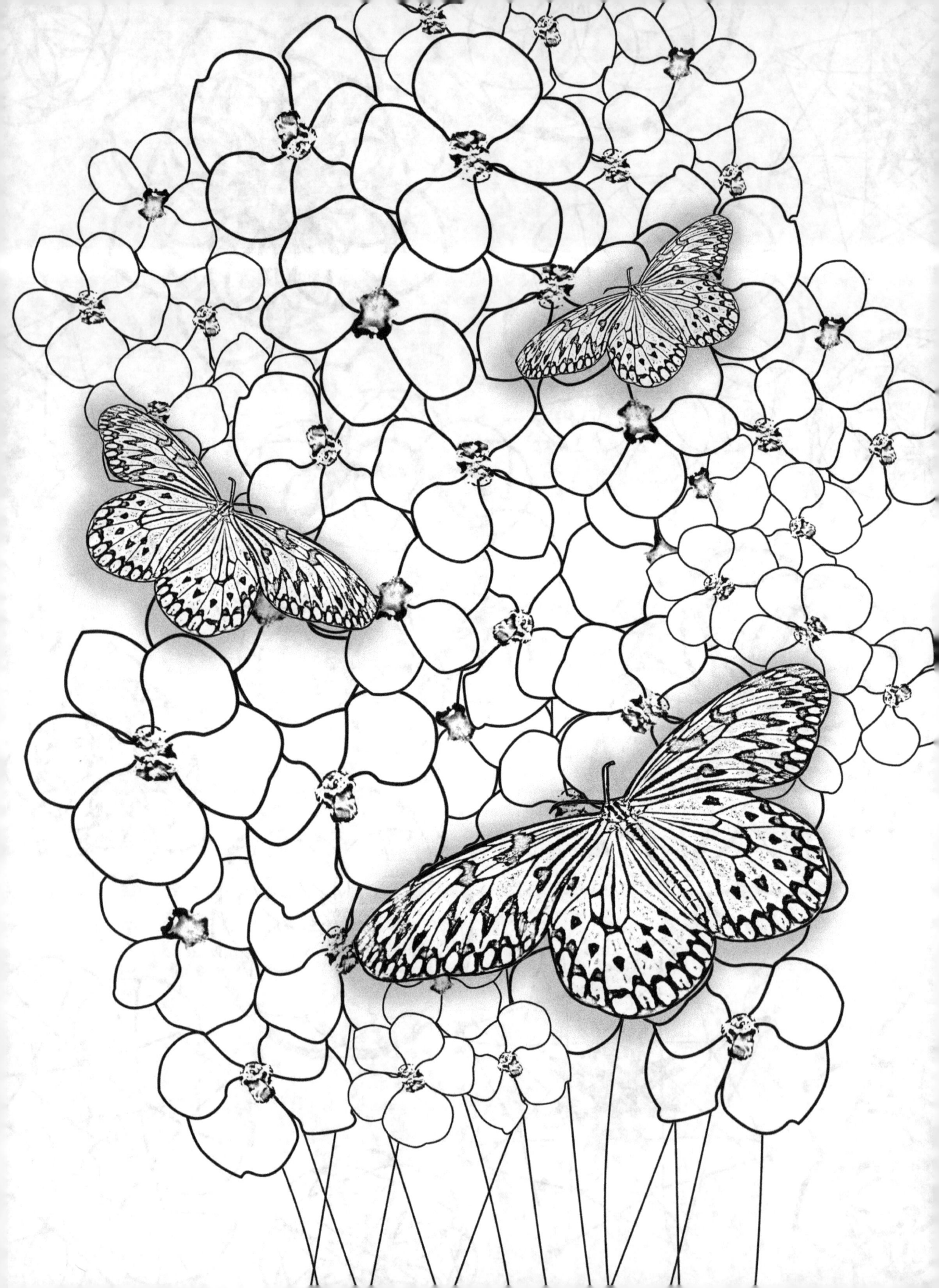

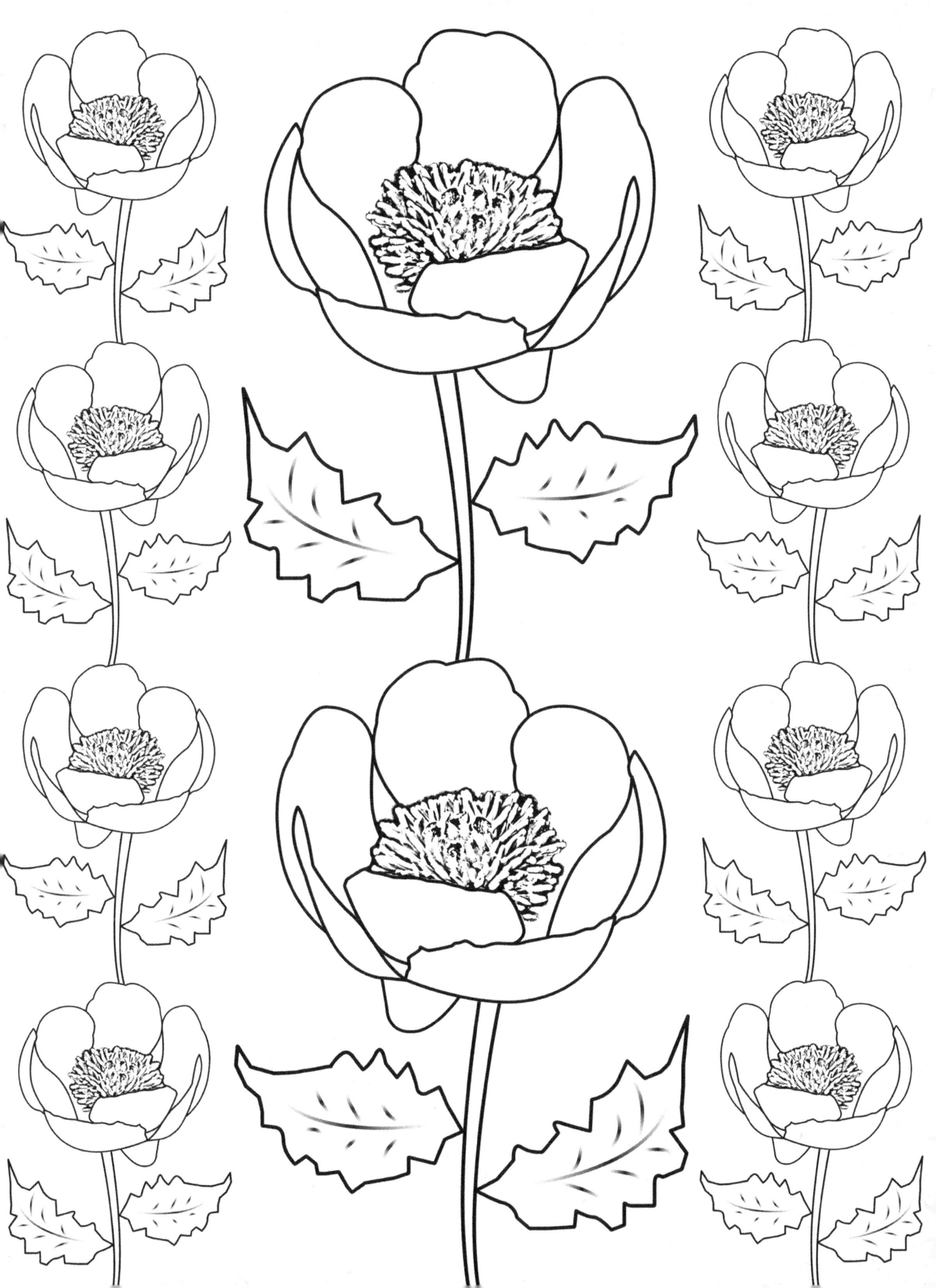

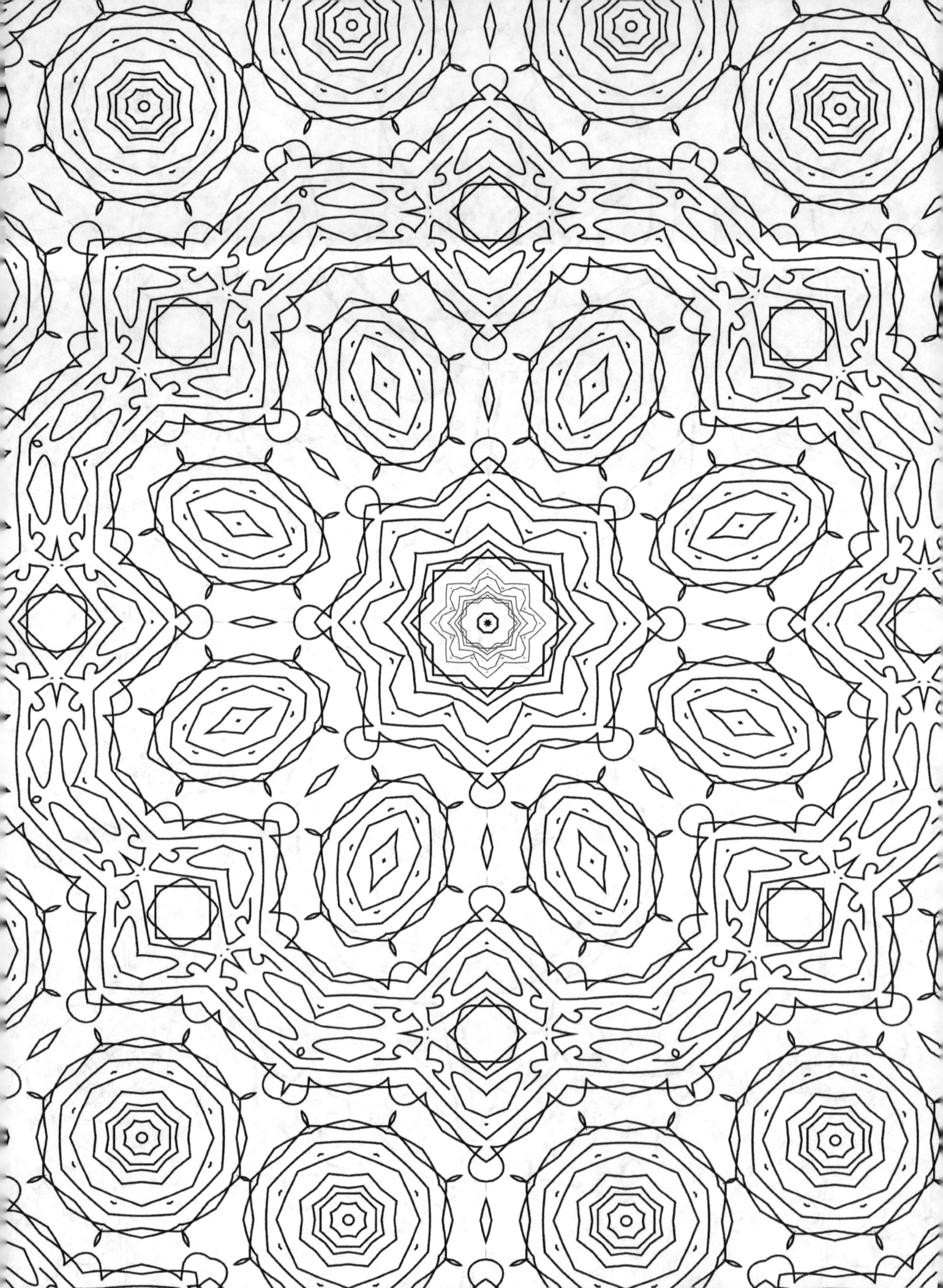

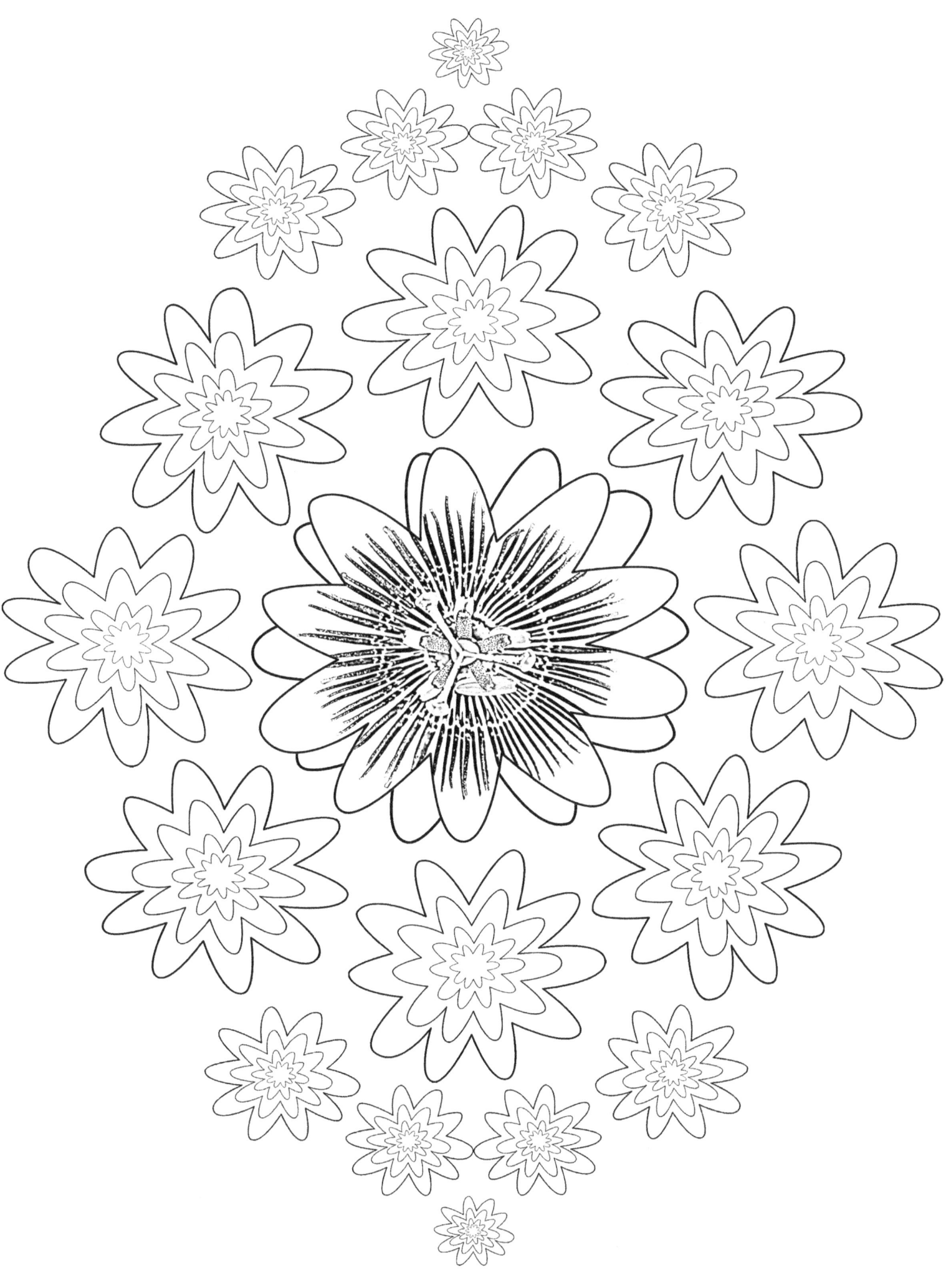

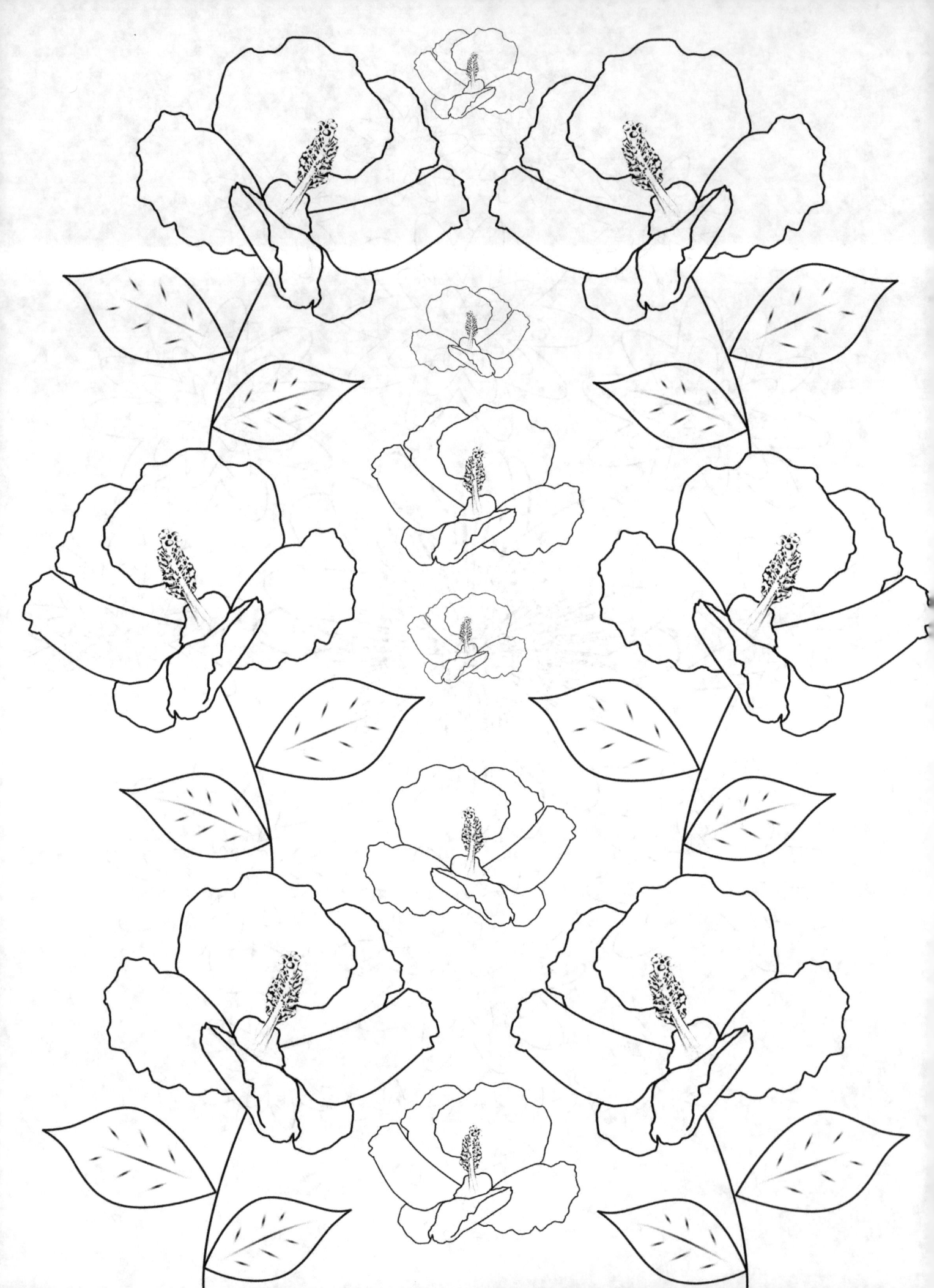

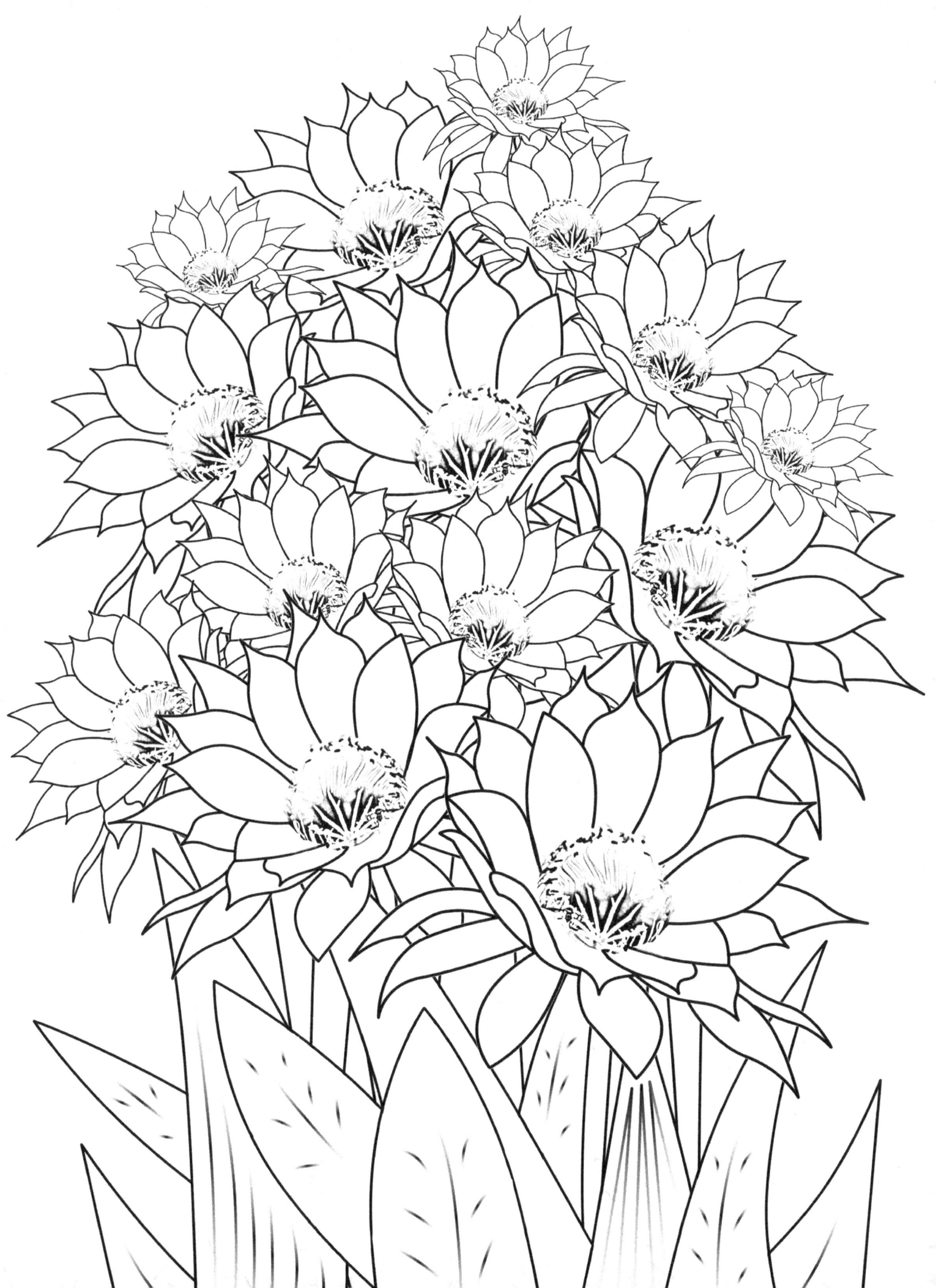

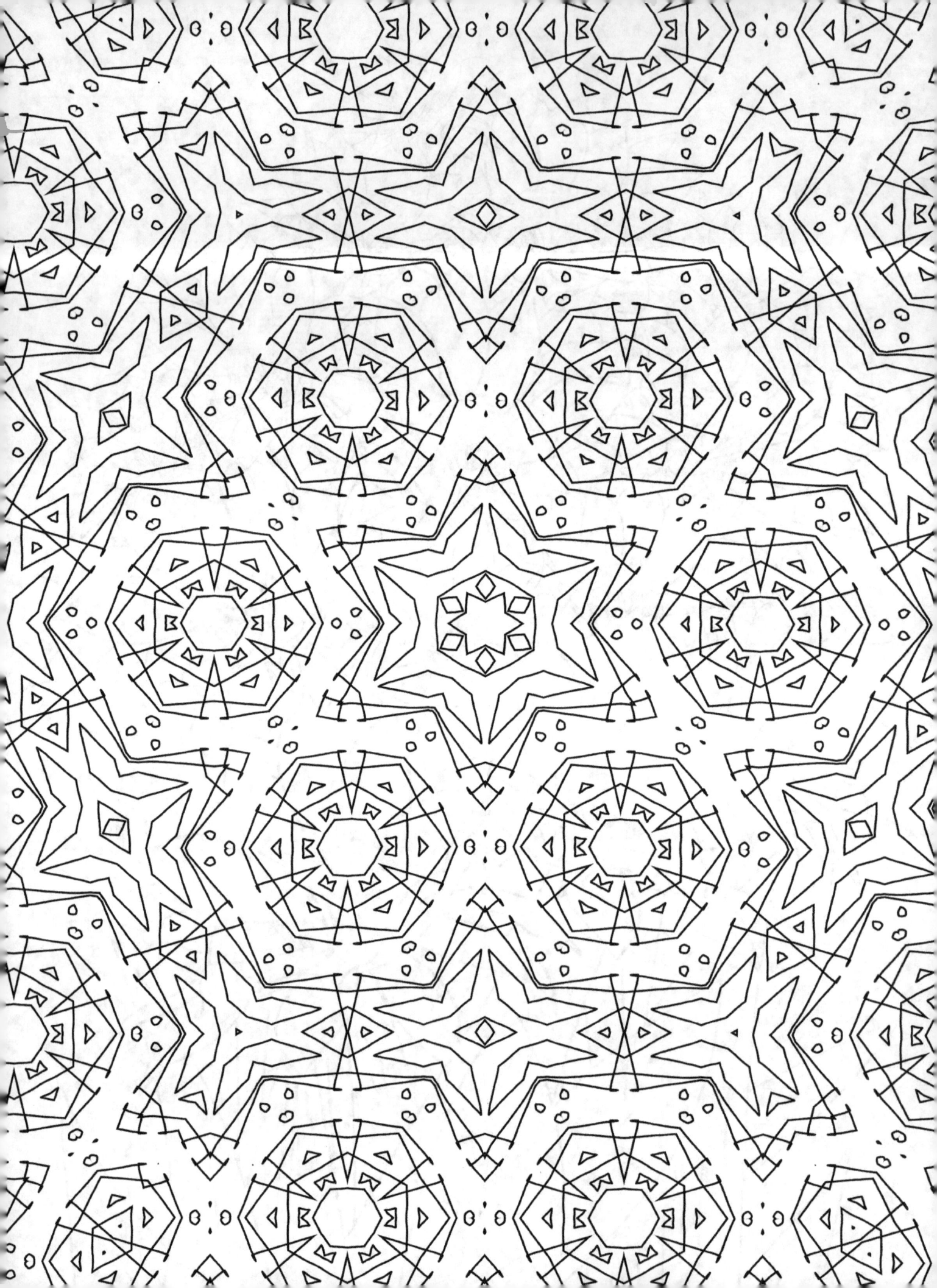

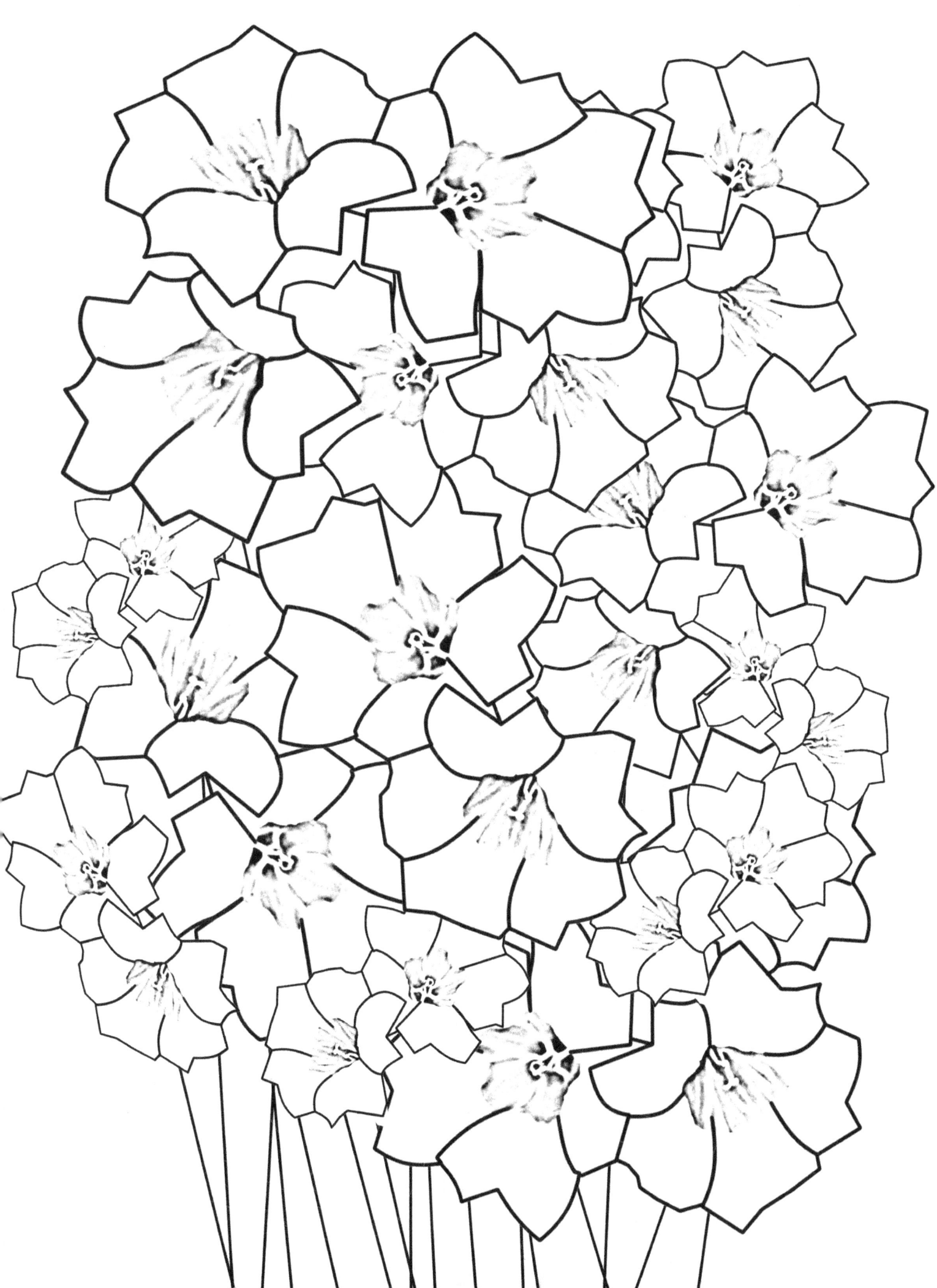

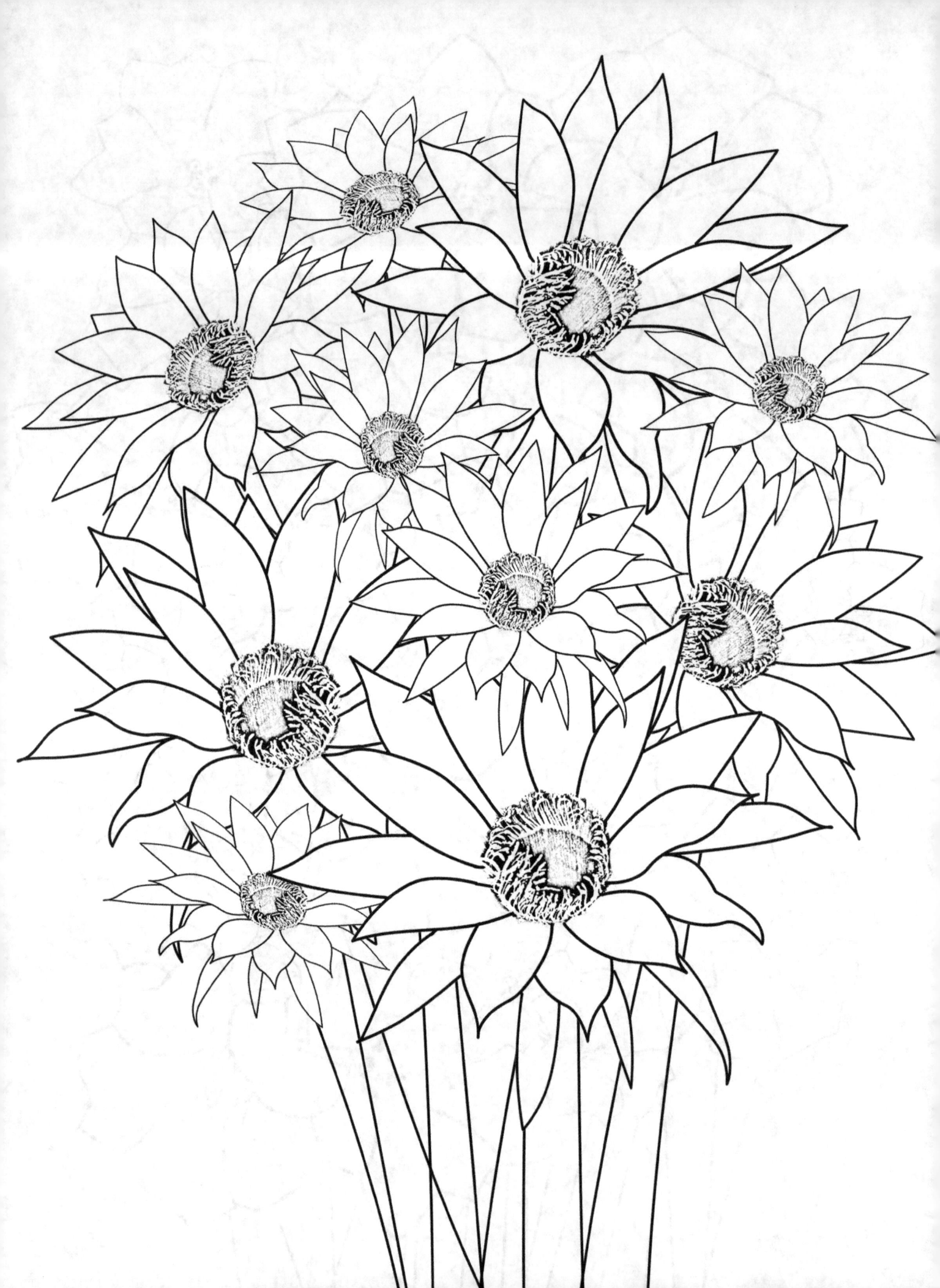

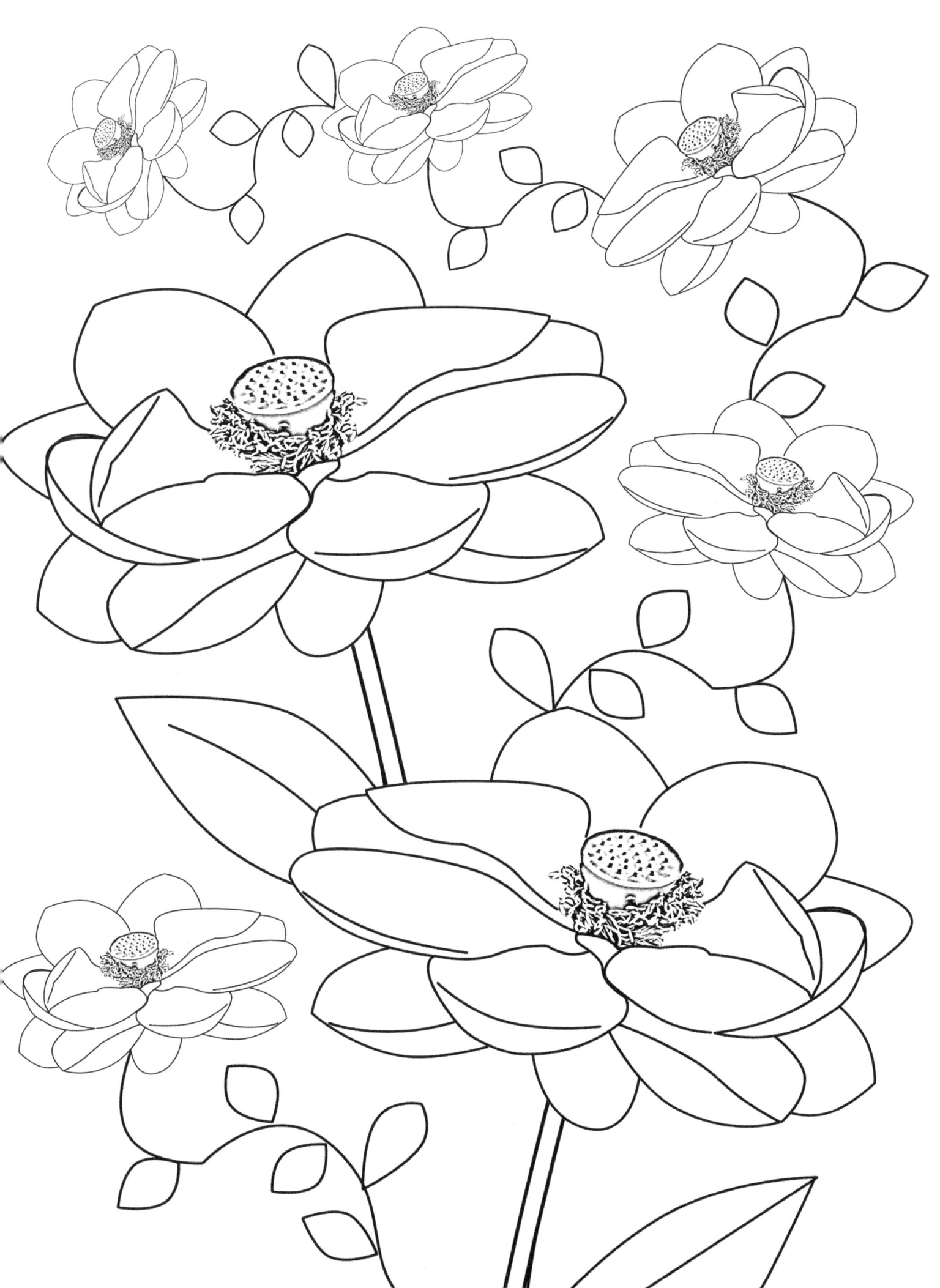

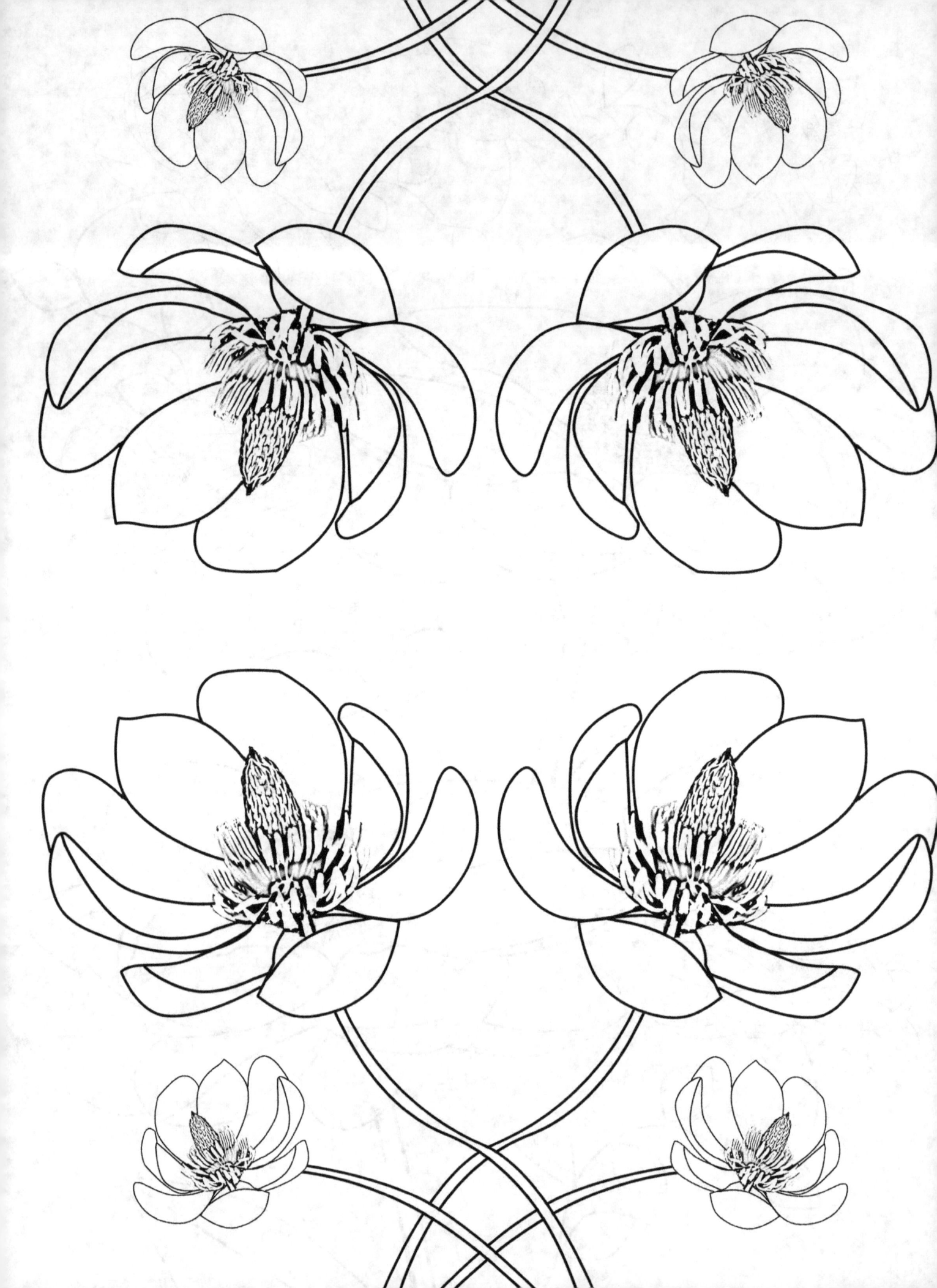

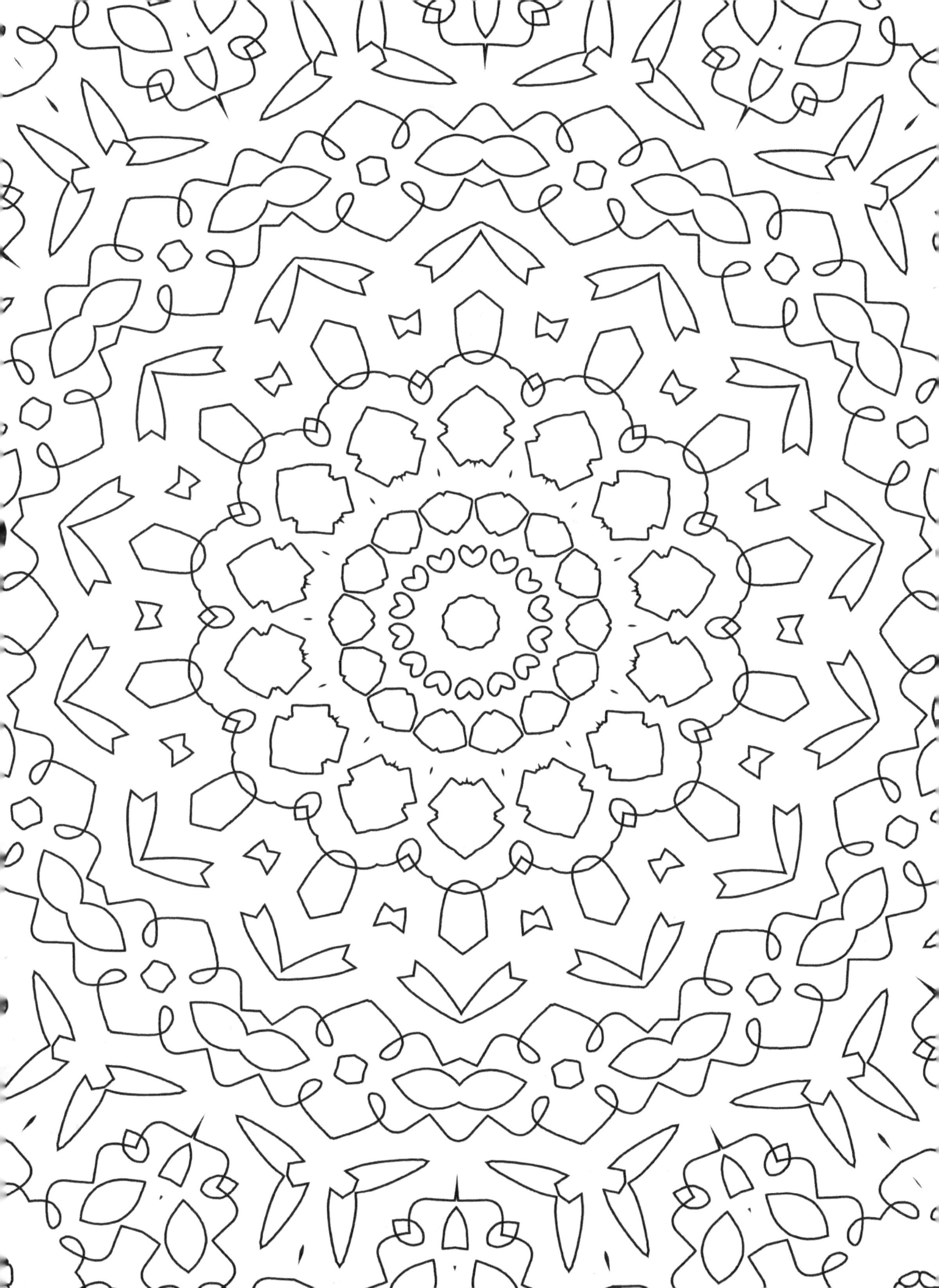

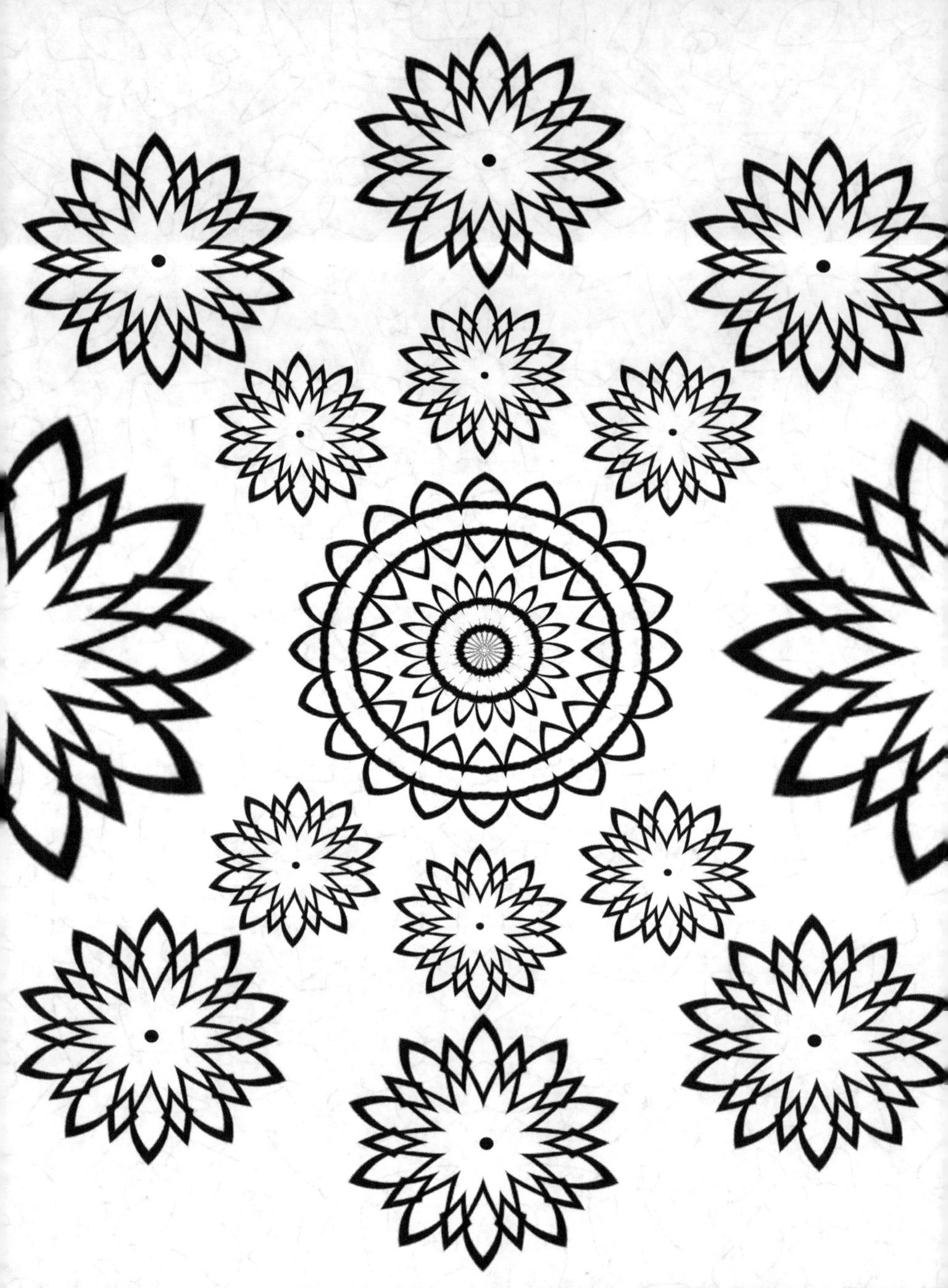

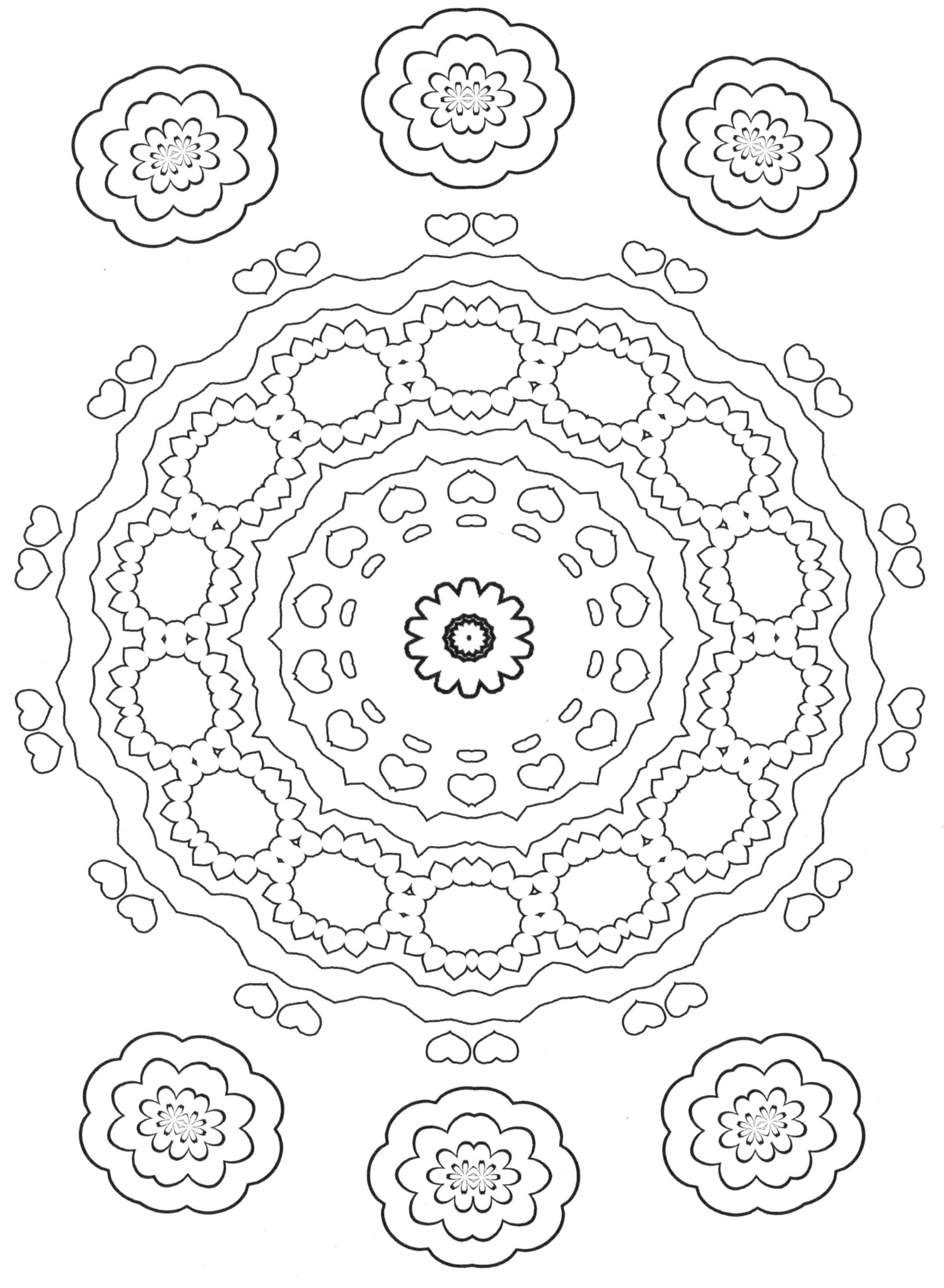

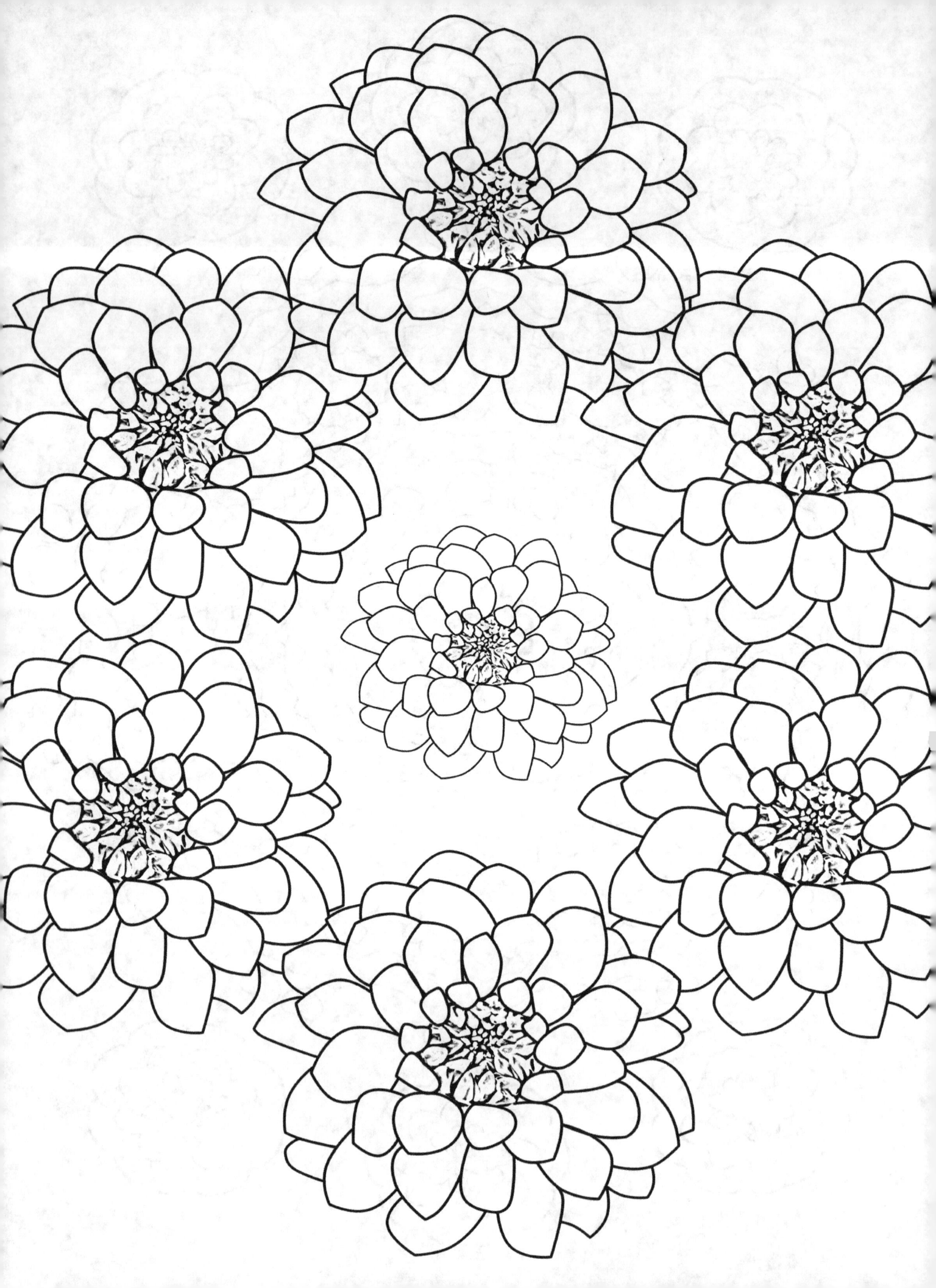

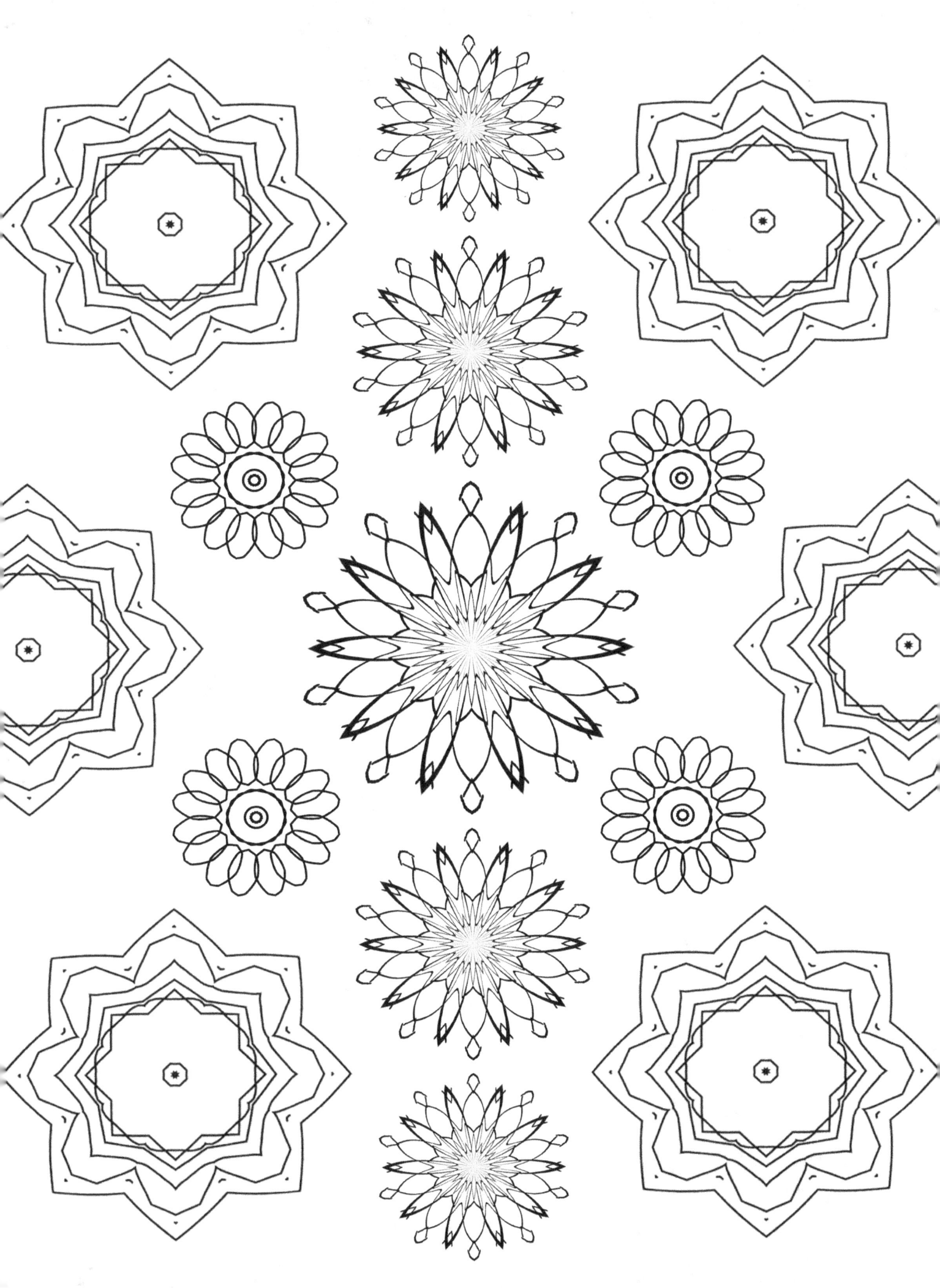

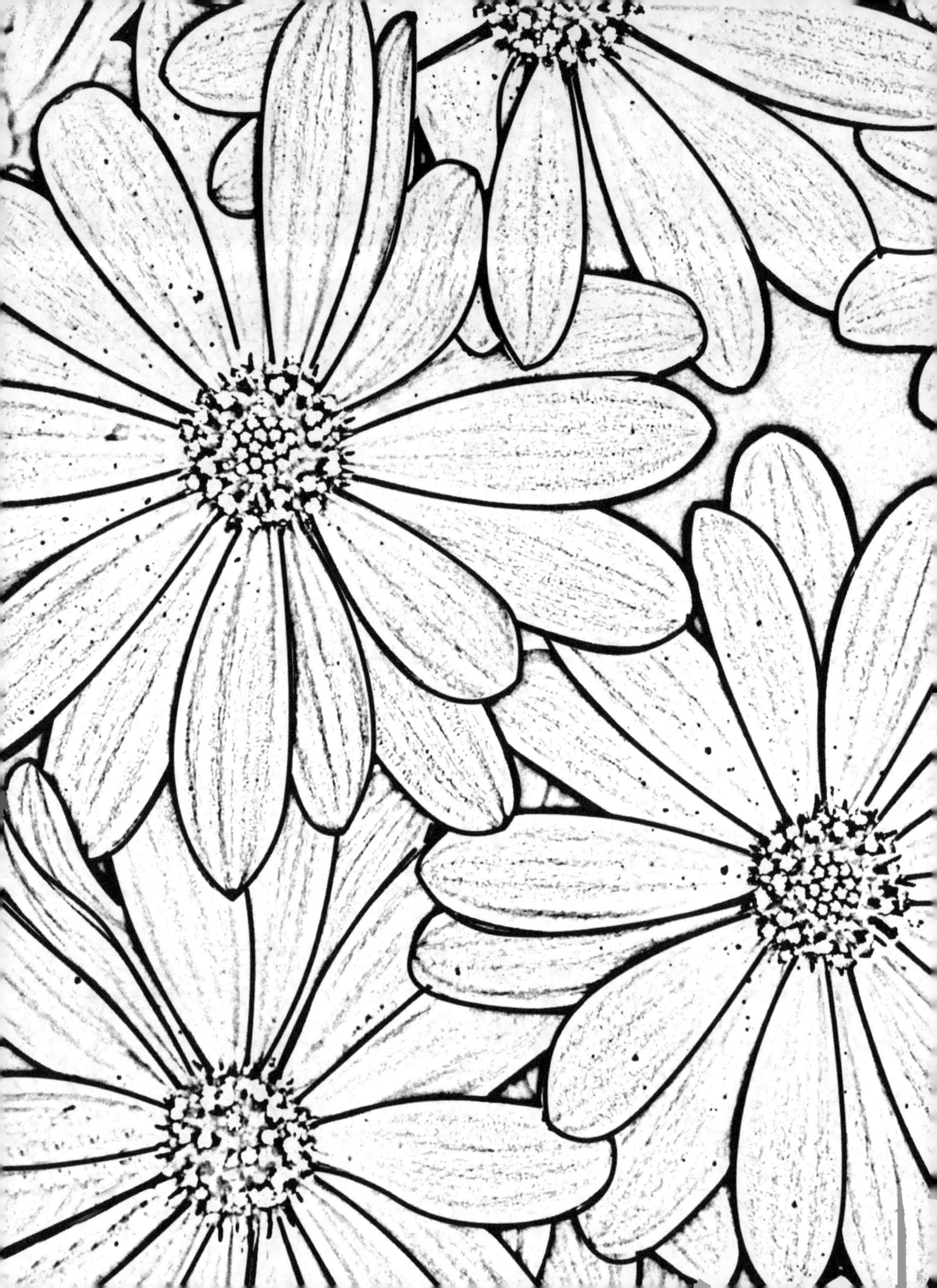

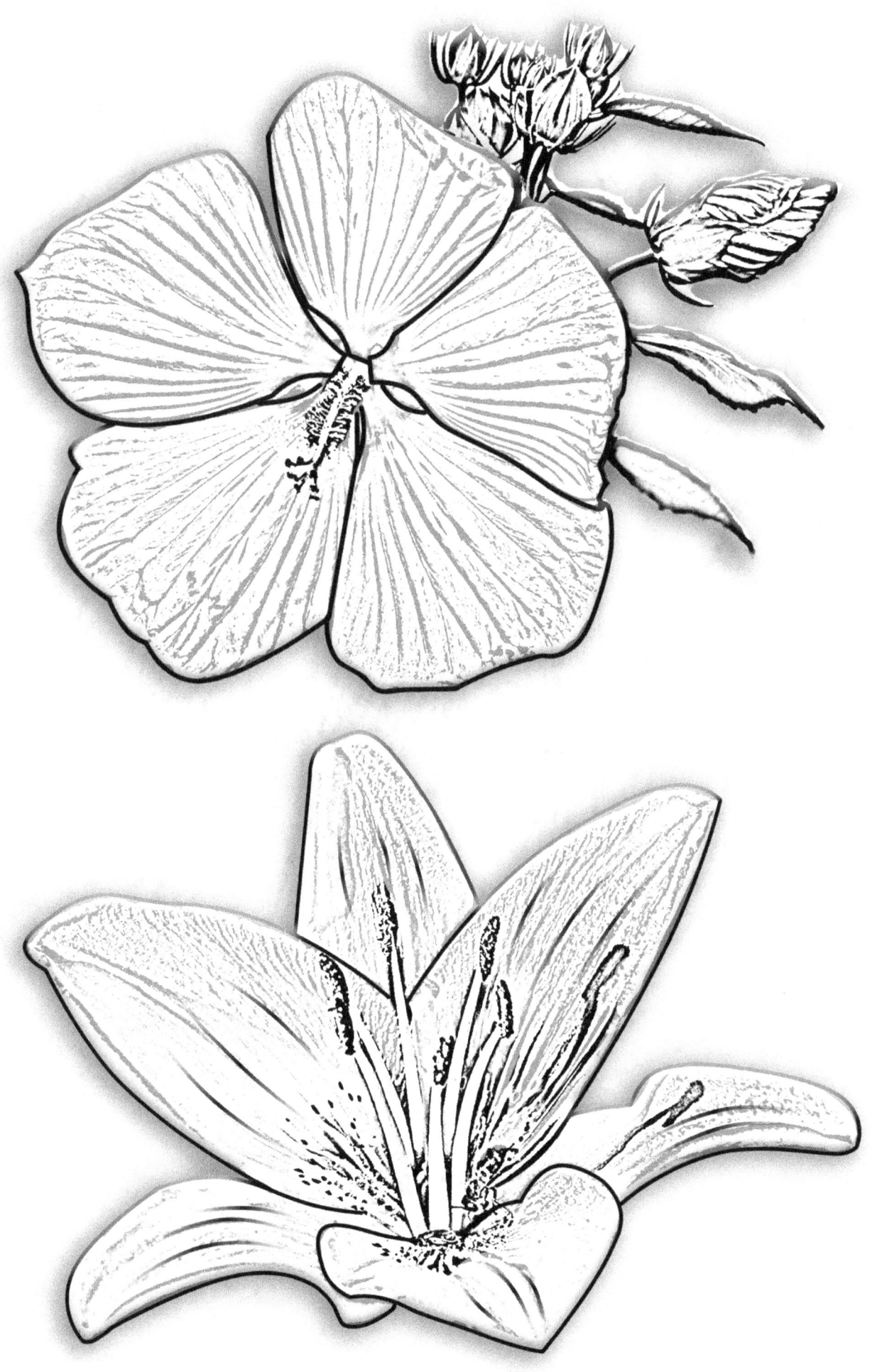

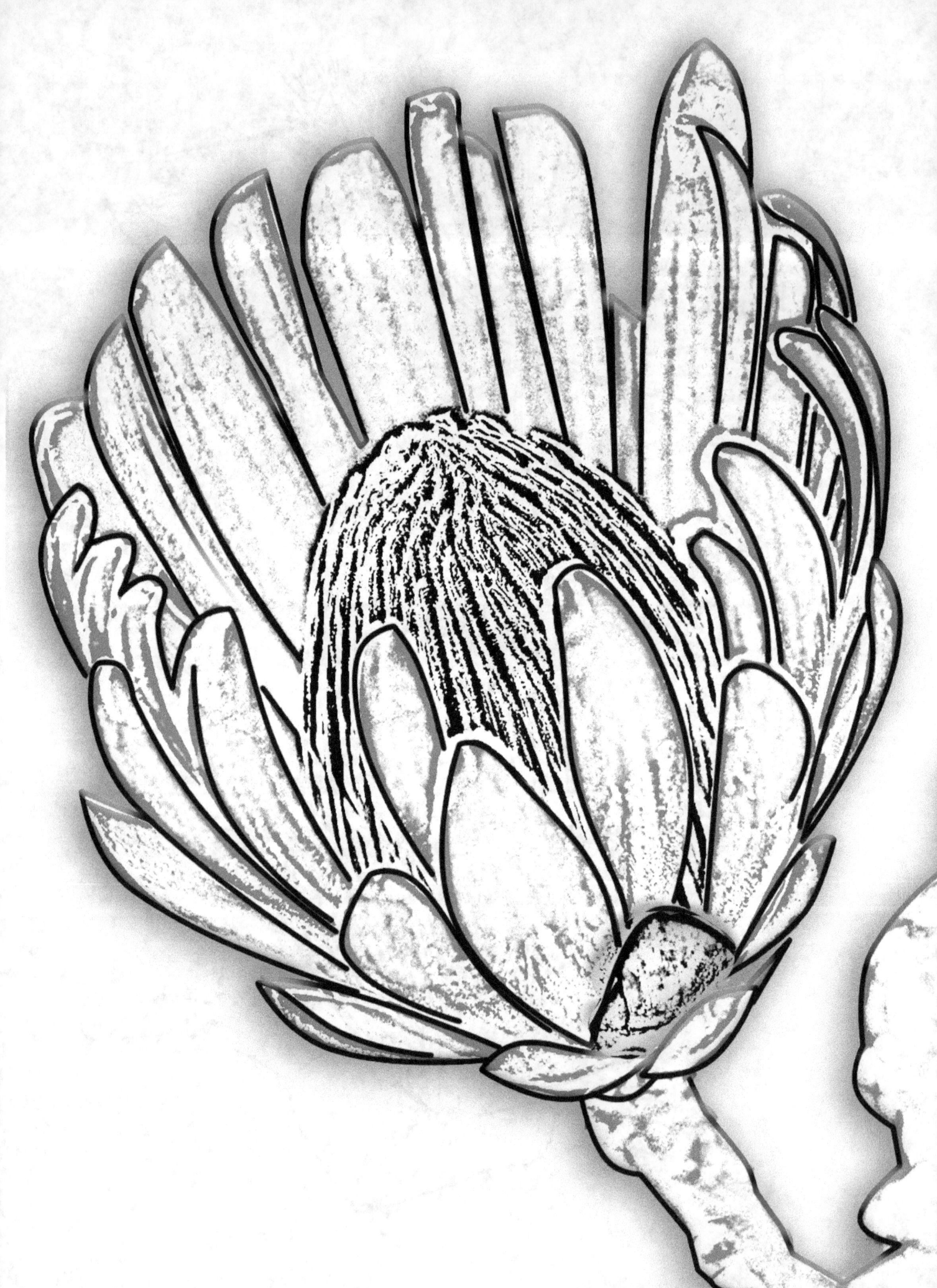

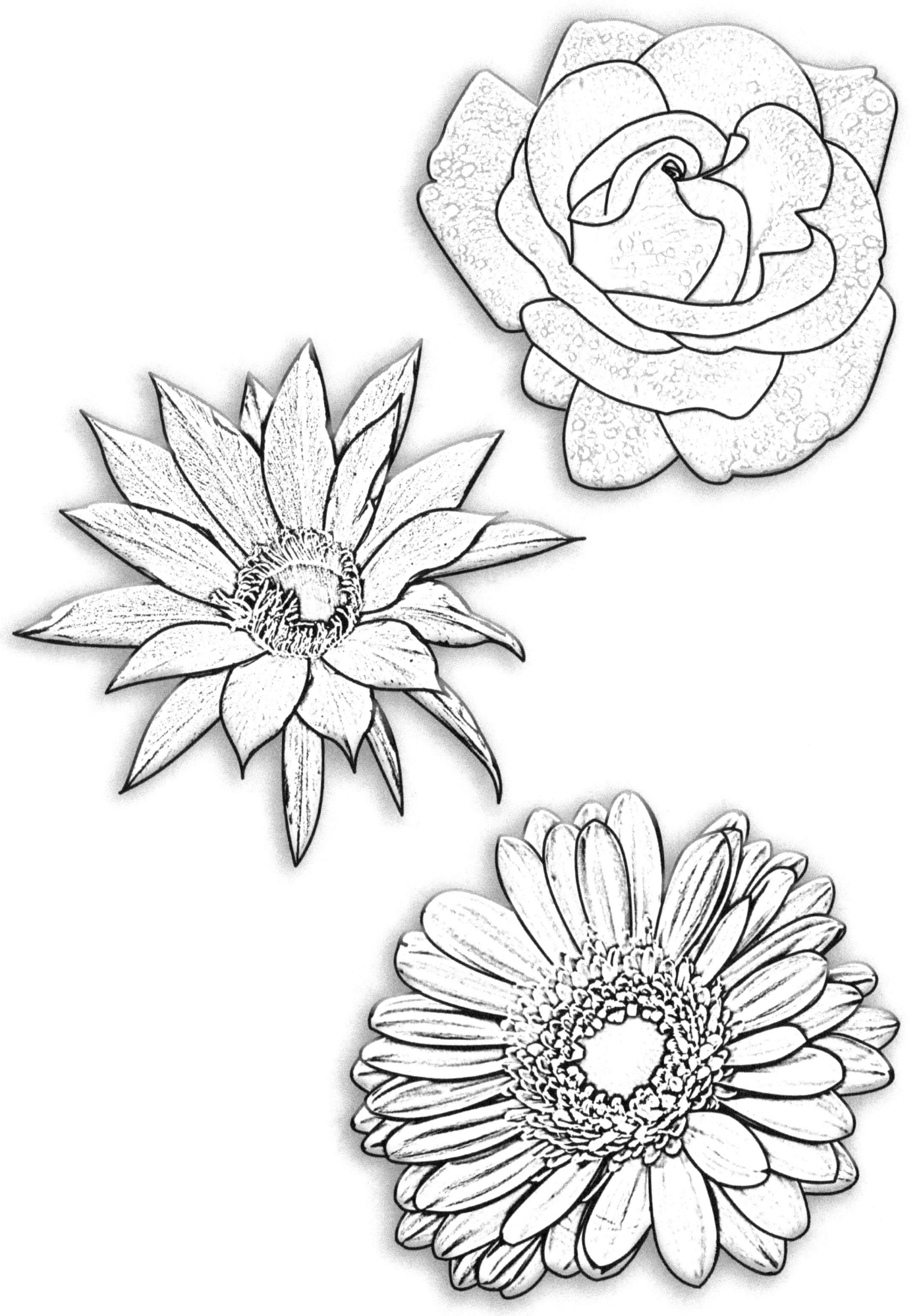

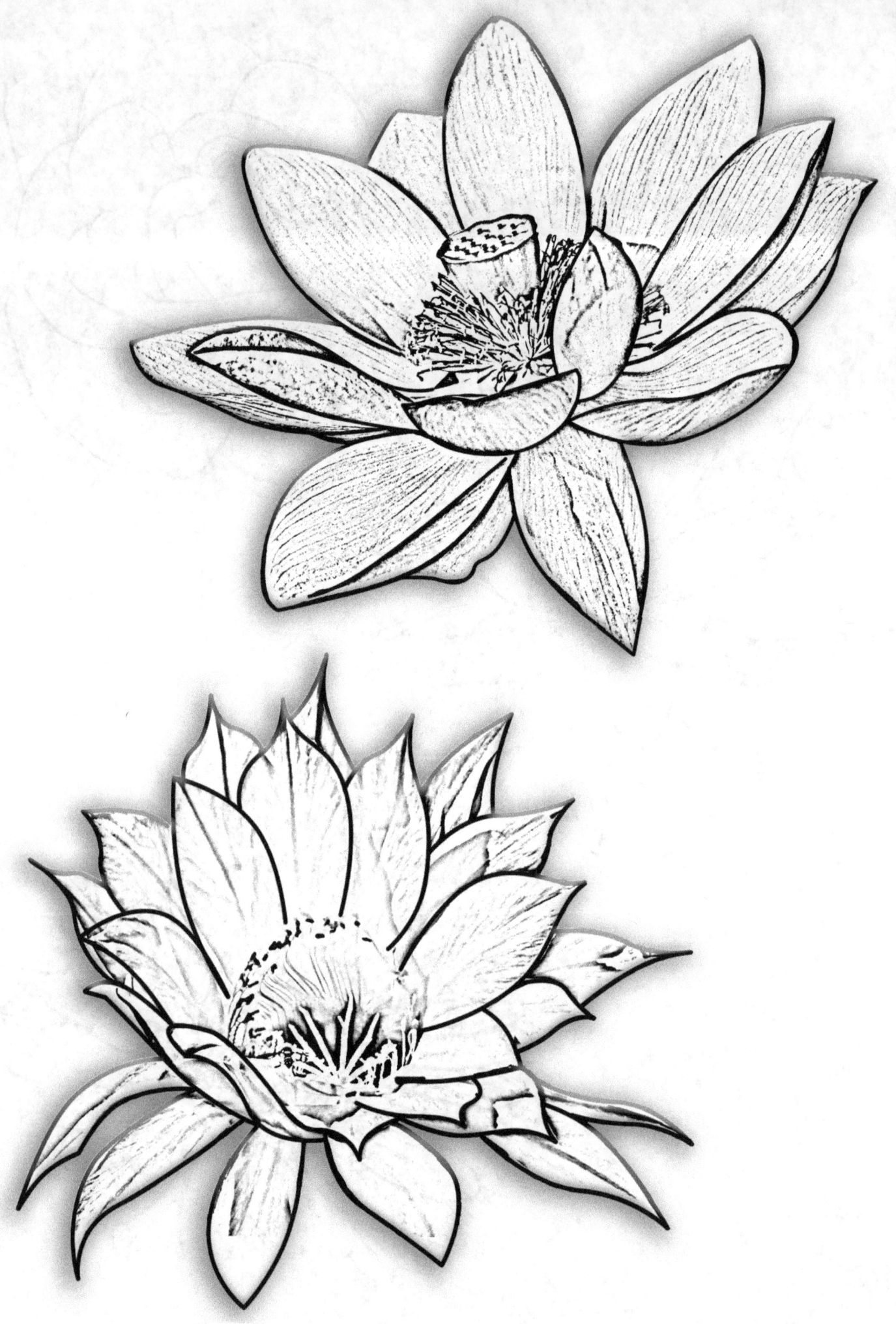

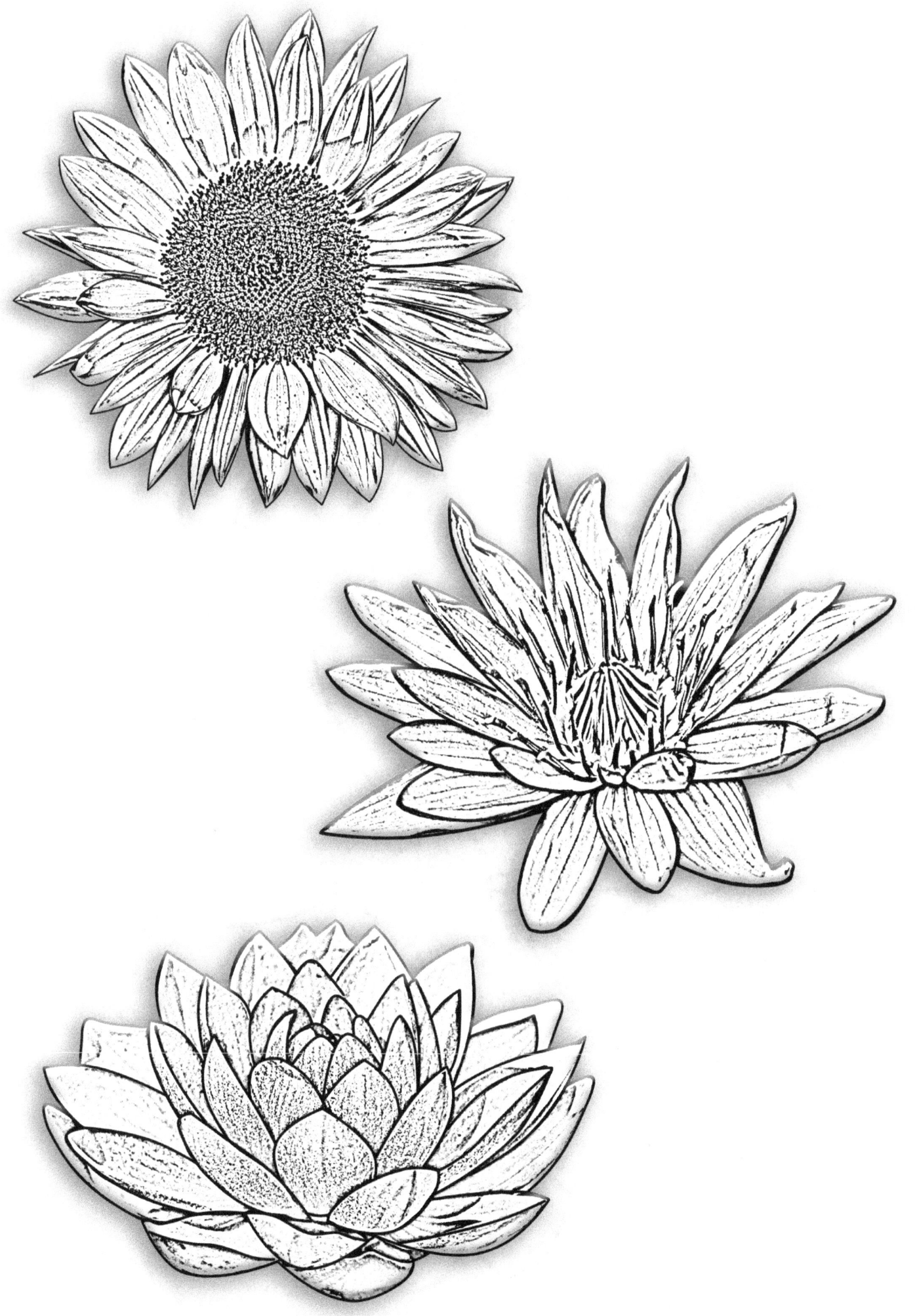

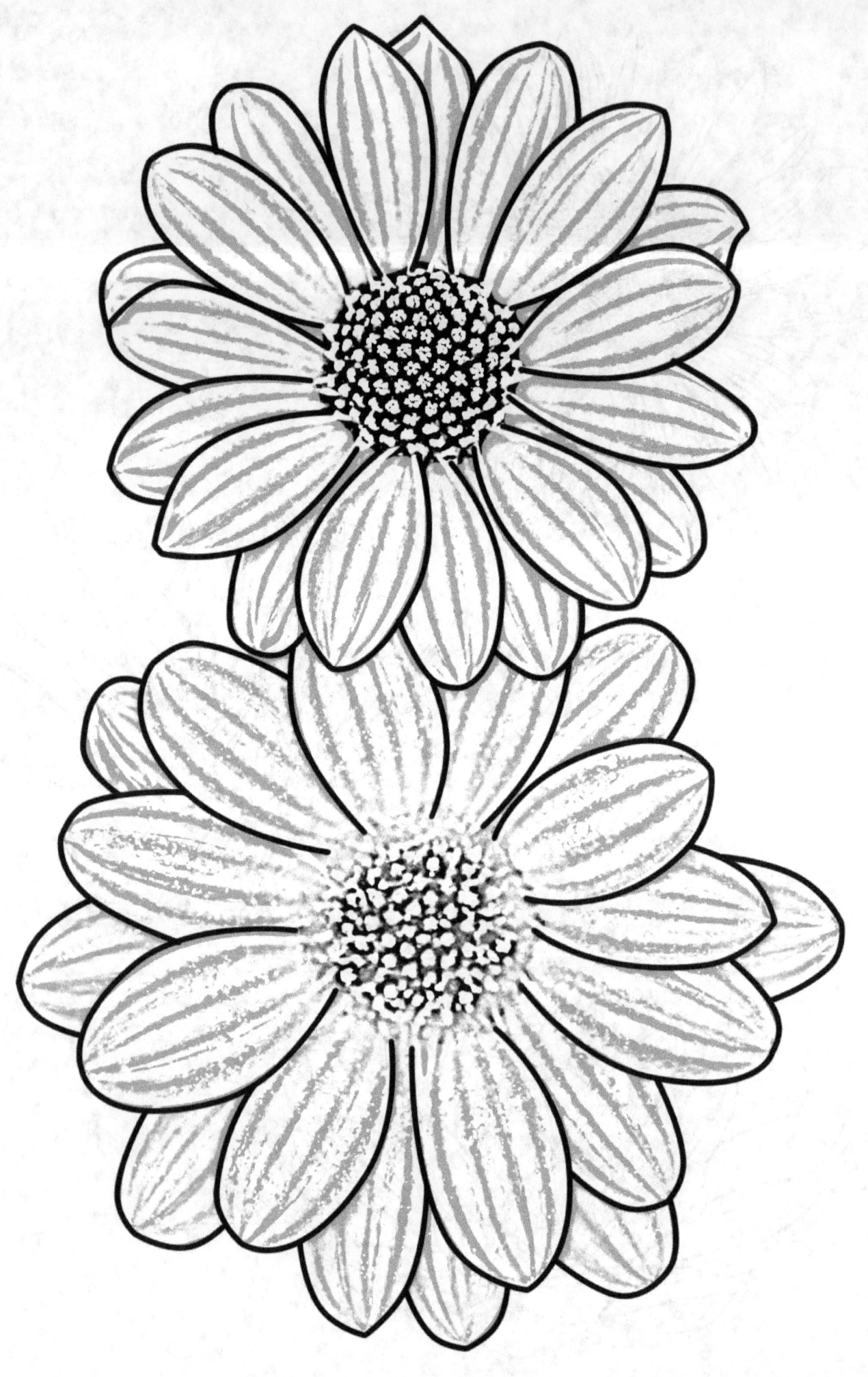

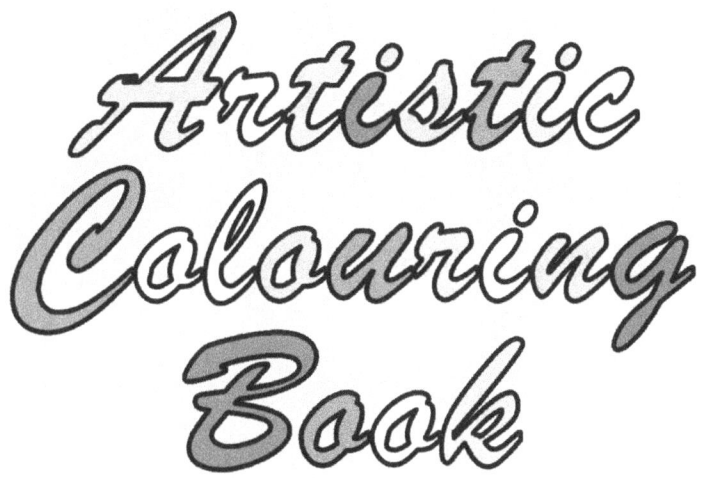

Artistic Colouring Book

by Milena Sladkova

www.ingramcontent.com/pod-product-compliance
Lightning Source LLC
Chambersburg PA
CBHW080528220526
45465CB00006B/2639